FACING
THE ISSUES 2

WILLIAM J. KRUTZA
AND PHILIP P. DI CICCO

Contemporary
Discussion Series

Baker Book House
Grand Rapids, Michigan 49506

Becaus...
help

Copyright 1969
by Baker Book House Company

ISBN: 0-8010-5326-9
Printed in the
United States of America

Ninth printing, February 1980

Why Discuss Issues?

TODAY'S CHURCH HAS AWAKENED to the issues of our day like the proverbial sleeping giant in a cave who took a nap in October and suddenly found it to be April. For a long time the church didn't evidence that it cared about what was going on in the world. The light has now dawned and the church is beginning to see that unless it speaks to the burning issues of our society, it will be left behind.

The church cannot afford to have the world, including the "now generation," pass it by. Individual churches and the church universal have a dynamic opportunity to say clearly to the world, "Now, as never before, the answers to life's perplexing problems need to be found in the Bible and in a vital relationship with Jesus Christ." You can show that Christianity does have something to say about such issues as poverty, race, violence, and art. You can show that the gospel touches every area of man's life, whether "spiritual" or "secular."

Why discuss issues? Basically because issues demand answers — answers that go to the heart of the issues. Our fast-paced age constantly presents new areas of living that demand the application of moral and scriptural guidelines. The world (and even many within the church) is bored with much of the theological jargon of the church. Why discuss issues?

3

e you and the members of your church cannot but be confronted with vital questions every day. You are "facing the issues" every day with neighbors, fellow-workers, friends and relatives.

Facing the issues and finding the answers is in the best New Testament tradition. Follow Christ in the gospels, and Paul in his letters, and you will find two of the greatest issue-facers the world has ever seen. Jesus confronted such problems as religious and racial bigotry (John 4), social unconcern (Matt. 23:23; 25:42, 43), poverty (Matt. 25:34-36; Luke 18:22), violence (Matt. 26:52), graft and greed (John 2:14-16). Paul dealt with questions of obeying governments and paying taxes (Rom. 13:1-7), marriage, sexual promiscuity and incest (I Cor. 7; I Cor. 5:1; I Cor. 6:15-19), idolatry (Acts 17:22-34), religious exclusivism and separatism (Acts 15; Gal. 2:11-16).

When discussing the issues facing the church and the world, we broaden our understanding and viewpoints by considering the ideas of others. Discussion ideas presented in this book are based on material with which you may agree or disagree. Various viewpoints are presented to stimulate group discussion, to challenge participation, to promote constructive thinking, to expose narrow-mindedness concerning Christian truth, and to open up areas for discussion to which Christians can interact.

The format of this book allows for varying viewpoints without giving preferences, so that those who participate can formulate their own conclusions through discussion. We feel that Christians will gain a fuller understanding of the issues and a clearer idea of the application of Scripture if they themselves "face the issues."

Effective witnesses to the world will demonstrate

4

the power of the Word of God by applying the fundamental principles of the Bible to everyday life. Christians must be fearless yet thoughtful in their application of God's Word. If Christians face up to the challenge as they discuss the issues, the gospel will penetrate more effectively into the world, and perhaps more people in the world will listen to what the church has to say.

How to Have
a Profitable Discussion

LECTURERS MAY FIND A GOLD MINE of helpful material in this book, but it is not intended as source material for lectures on the issues that face Christians today. It is rather intended to excite people to tackle some of the pressing issues of our day. The way this book is put together — first stating what others have already said on the issues, followed by Scripture that applies to the subjects, and then with the "What Do You Say?" section — will create mind-challenging situations in which people can express their views and hopefully come up with genuine Christian application and action. To facilitate this process we offer the following suggestions:

Each participant should have a copy of "Facing the Issues." This will allow for pre-discussion study of the materials and time to do additional research. The more each participant thinks through the materials, the more profitable will his or her contributions be in the discussion sessions.

Keep each discussion centered upon the theme of the materials presented in that particular discussion. A discussion that drifts to subjects unrelated to the theme usually does not accomplish much in the thinking of the participants. Save other topics for future discussions. Possibly have one member of the discussion group take notes on subjects to be discussed at another time. More than ample material is included in each chapter.

Have each member of the group participate in each discussion. It is easy to let one or two people do all the talking, but this may not be of the greatest benefit to those in the discussion group. The discussion leader should guard against this and consciously ask others to voice their opinions or give additional information. Some silent members of the group may have the best ideas to contribute because they have been thinking them through while the others have been talking. All those who have ideas should be allowed to express them before going on to the next question.

Use the printed materials as a guide, not as a needed-to-be-covered curriculum. The material in this book is given as a springboard for constructive discussion. The discussion questions need not be taken in the order given. Nor is it necessary to seek answers to all of the questions. If a question does not fit your particular situation or locale, go to the others or rephrase the question to make it relevant to your situation.

If your group gets wound up on one or two questions, don't insist on going further. Save the remainder of the questions for the next discussion session or for an after-meeting coffee time.

Seek to develop positive, workable solutions to the issues. We already know that the issues are controversial. If they weren't, they would not have been included in this book. Some might be tempted to give quick and easy solutions — often negative ones to the issues in this book. Anyone can be negative. Anyone can throw up his arms and say the church

7

has no business dabbling in this or that issue. Anyone can condemn others who have tried to give answers to these issues. But it takes considerable grace, wisdom, charity, and honesty to offer solutions that will give positive guidance to the members of the discussion group who want to face the issues realistically.

Most issues do not have cut-and-dried solutions. It may take considerable thought and discussion to arrive at adequate answers. You will find that on some of the issues the only suitable solution is a consensus of opinion. On others, your group will come up with dynamic answers and actions. In each case, the authors sincerely hope that the end result will produce Christian solutions that apply to the various issues as they present themselves in local communities and in the nation. As group members discuss these issues, and think through toward positive answers, they will be better equipped to face the world where these issues are constantly raised.

Contents

Is It Right to Tax Churches?   1

CHURCHES IN THE UNITED STATES FACE the issue of taxation in a more serious way than at any other time in their history. The rising need for public services, the growing demands on governments both federal and local, bring the issue to the fore. The United States Congress is considering several bills which include tax reform measures that relate to taxing certain church-related assets.

Traditionally, churches in America have not been taxed. Among other reasons the early founders did not want to interfere with religion and the "free exercise thereof." As churches now amass great amounts of property and capital, the issue has been raised. Now, during a period when the demands on governments have increased to phenomenal proportions, the wealth of the churches has come under intensive scrutiny.

Church wealth and the worth of church-related enterprises is not known accurately because no adequate auditing system has even been set up. Estimates of church wealth vary. One estimate puts the value of church held properties and investments at a little over $100 billion. Such properties could yield the government substantial tax revenue. Some estimates go as high as $2.2 billion to local, state, and federal treasuries yearly. While the exact figures cannot be known, examples of church wealth abound. For instance, recently the Poor Sisters of Mishawaka, Indiana, who have a little over 500 professed members, disclosed a net worth of $86 million. This came to light because they sought to float a loan of $4.5 million from the public through notes. In 1960, the Knights of Columbus disclosed assets of $162 million.

The vast amount of money tied up in churches is not merely that invested in places of worship and schools, but in financial holdings in a diverse number of business enterprises. Income, unrelated to the main function of religion comes into church treasuries through such enterprises as girdle factories, large hotels, apartment houses, garbage disposal dumps, trading stamps, fruitcake sales, baseball stadiums — and many other business ventures!

What makes all this "extra-curricular" activity suspect to many people is that most of these activities are carried on with tax advantages through church-connected exemptions, even though such businesses are in direct competition with commercial organizations that pay normal taxes.

One example of how this may work is through "leaseback" arrangements. A church buys business property on credit and then leases it back to the original owner. The rentals are tax-exempt and yield the church an income which helps pay off the loan balance. The original owner gets both the proceeds from the sale and the usual operating profits.

Church leaders who have used this kind of loophole have argued that the good works and general benefits of churches in the community justify such arrangements — especially since churches are financing colleges, hospitals, and missionary work. Critics do not see it this way. When as much as 30 per cent

churches 7½%

of the land in the United States is tax-exempt (churches own about 25% of that total, or about $80 billion worth), doubts arise whether churches are really paying their way.

Extensive studies have been made of exempt properties in various places. In Washington, D.C., 609 acres of religious land in 1966 were valued at $131 million, 4.6 per cent of all land in Washington, D.C., is exempt. Protestants account for 57 per cent of these exemptions, based on 326 churches valued at $75 million. If all denominational-owned holdings such as hospitals, cemeteries, and charitable organizations were added, the valuation would reach $85 million.

Depending on how you define "church," studies in other cities indicate that 17 per cent of all property in Maryland, 18 per cent in New Jersey, and 16 per cent in Baltimore is church-owned.

Church wealth in the past few years has shown signs of growing rather than diminishing, especially within the Roman Catholic Church. The Roman Catholic Church, according to one expert, owns over $11 billion worth of tax-exempt land and buildings in the U.S. A few examples are given by Fred R. Zepp, in an article in the *Christian Herald:* "A survey of conditions in Buffalo has found that in 58 years Catholic properties rose from 43 to 71 per cent of the total exempt, increasing 367 per cent while Protestant valuations fell 24.5 per cent.

"In Denver, where the Catholic Church owned 14 per cent of all religious property in 1906, it owned 39 per cent in 1964; . . . In the nation's capital, where they comprise 22 per cent of the population Roman Catholics account for 58 per cent of the religiously owned — and tax exempt — property."[1]

Many wonder whether churches are getting off

too easily while building empires inconsistent with their stated purposes. Eugene Carson Blake, Executive Secretary of the World Council of Churches, has for a long time considered exemption for churches a too-much abused privilege and has advocated taxing churches. He has predicted that if the practice of allowing churches to profit from unrelated business ventures is retained with reasonable good management, that churches will be able to control the whole economy of the nation within a predictable time. Other religious leaders have warned that the churches in America may be in danger of "gaining the whole world and losing its own soul."

Various denominations differ as to the degree that churches should be taxed. Some feel that all church assets should be taxed; others feel only those buildings, land or organizations not directly related to the function of the church should be taxed. The question of what is a church function and what can be considered "charitable" is now open to question. It is primarily the unrelated business undertakings that come in direct competition with other businesses that causes such concern. Most Protestants feel that these types of arrangements at least should be taxed like other businesses.

"The government should look at the source of the income (commercial undertakings) rather than the use to which it is put (missions, schools, welfare) in determining whether to tax it."[2]

A *Christianity Today* editorial stated: "It is high time for all churches to report their incomes and pay taxes on business profits. Church land and buildings used specifically for religious and educational purposes should remain tax free, along with those of other eleemosynary institutions. But the church must not shirk its responsibility to pay taxes on business

14 * of, for, derived from, or dependent on charity

ventures on the same basis as private enterprisers."[3]

Some churches are so concerned about this issue that they are beginning to make contributions to the government in lieu of taxes. These churches have done this on the grounds that they receive vital services such as fire and police protection and owe this to their communities. Many feel that the church should be a positive benefit rather than a burden on society.

The 175th General Assembly of the Presbyterian Church, U.S.A. approved a statement that any favored tax position was a "hindrance to the fulfilling of the church's mission." It warned that accepting such "special privileges" renders the church's "witness ambiguous." It urged that the church try to "extricate itself from the position of being obligated, or seeming to be obligated, to the state by virtue of special tax privileges extended to it."[4]

Some have raised a constitutional question on the issue. The well publicized atheist, Madelyn O'Hair sought to force the issue by a suit she filed in Maryland. She lost the suit, but continues to advocate forcing the churches to pay taxes. Her motives however are poles apart from most religious leaders.

She contends that because churches do not pay taxes she must pay more than her fair share. This, she says, violates the First Amendment ban on laws permitting or condoning the establishment of religion and denies her of her property without due process of law. Mrs. O'Hair frankly told newsmen that churches were "leeches on society," and that she was determined to make them pay taxes.

Many feel that churches will have to participate more in bearing the tax share, not only because of the changing economic situation, but because of the changing mood of both governments and populace.

Growing resentment, not only among outspoken atheists, but among working people who already feel their taxes are too high may be a future hindrance to the church's mission. Elwyn A. Smith wrote in *The Christian Century:* "If the church intends to be seriously religious as well as inevitably secular, it should make its uniquely religious activities as independent of government as possible, performing certain types of action without aid or privilege from government. If a church cannot pay its taxes on its present worship properties now, it should cut those assets to the point where it can afford them. I do not say that the church should pay taxes on all assets and income tomorrow; I say rather that it should start moving immediately toward a position where it can maintain itself without dependence on tax exemption, much less on subsidies."[5]

There are many who feel that the power to tax is the power to destroy and that permitting taxation might enable a subtle form of persecution of churches at a future time. Others feel that if and when a government wanted to destroy the churches it could do so apart from taxation. It is both possible and probable that if taxes were levied on churches it would be an unbearable burden on some churches, almost forcing them to close. This would be true of small churches which struggle to pay a pastor and building rent, and for large congregations who have over-extended their resources.

The Christian Century aptly summarizes some of the vital issues of this subject in its review of D. B. Robertson's book, *Should Churches Be Taxed?*

"Doesn't tax exemption imply a reciprocal obligation on the part of the churches to report their financial condition to the public? If they participate in the benefits of the social order, don't the churches have an obligation to help pay its costs beginning with fire and police protection? Would payment of taxes extinguish weak congregations and if so would that be a bad thing? Is it an adequate compromise for churches voluntarily to give the local taxing authority an amount equal to all or part of the taxes they would pay if taxation of churches became compulsory? If land used for buildings intended only for worship is exempt, what about income-producing property?"[6]

WHAT DOES THE BIBLE SAY?

"And when they were come to Capernaum, they that received tribute money came to Peter, and said, Doth not your master pay tribute? He saith, Yes. And when he was come into the house, Jesus prevented him, saying, What thinkest thou, Simon? of whom do the kings of the earth take custom or tribute? Of their own children, or of strangers? Peter saith unto him, Of strangers. Jesus saith unto him, Then are the children free. Nothwithstanding, lest we should offend them, go thou to the sea, and cast an hook, and take up the fish that first cometh up; and when thou hast opened its mouth, thou shalt find a piece of money: that take, and give unto them for me and thee" (Matt. 17:24-27).

"Tell us, therefore, What thinkest thou? Is it lawful to give tribute unto Caesar, or not? But Jesus perceived their wickedness, and said, Why tempt ye me, ye hypocrites? Show me the tribute money. And they brought unto him a penny. And he saith unto them, Whose is this image and superscription? They say unto him, Caesar's. Then saith he unto them, Render, therefore, unto Caesar the things which are Caesar's; and unto

God, the things that are God's (Matt. 22:17-21).

"For for this cause pay ye tribute also; for they are God's ministers, attending continually upon this very thing. Render therefore to all their dues: tribute to whom tribute is due; custom to whom custom; fear to whom fear, honor to whom honor" (Rom. 13:6, 7).

WHAT DO YOU SAY?

1. Is there any basis in Scripture for exempting churches from taxes? Is Jesus' statement about "rendering unto Caesar" applicable to the question of taxing churches?

2. Was Jesus' willingness to pay taxes, since He was considered a religious teacher, an indication that religious groups should not be exempted?

3. Should churches begin making contributions "in lieu of taxes" in order to show good faith? Could the establishment of such a precedent eventually bring harm to churches?

4. Should churches be taxed for income received from "unrelated" sources, such as business enterprises and rentals? If so, should it be on the same basis as other business enterprises?

5. How can a church prepare for the possibility of having to pay taxes at some future time?

6. In what sense would churches have a more effective witness if they were not obligated to the state because of tax exemption? Is there any way that present exemptions to churches are detrimental to the image of the church?

7. What factors should be taken into consideration in deciding whether churches should be taxed?

Is there any reason they should receive special treatment? What are they?

8. How much of a church's financial affairs should be reported to the government? Why?

9. Is the basis for tax exemption as it developed in the United States still a valid one? Does exemption from taxes affect the doctrine of separation of church and state as understood in the United States?

10. Since the church is composed of individuals who have donated out of their already taxed income, would it be fair to tax income received as offerings?

11. Does the privilege of being able to deduct contributions to churches on a person's income tax return relate to the question of taxing churches? Why should religious people be favored in this way by the state?

12. Is the argument that the church does good works and is beneficial to society a valid argument for giving churches tax relief? Why or why not?

13. Since it is the affluence of churches in our present day that is bringing up the question of taxing this enormous wealth, would it be wise for churches to reduce their wealth?

14. What can churches do to avoid the accusation of amassing wealth to the exclusion of helping the poor? Should churches pay "reparations" for their past unconcern for underprivileged groups?

Notes

1. Fred R. Zepp, "Should Church Property Be Taxed?" *Christian Herald,* January 1966. Reprinted by permission.

2. *Ibid.*

3. "The Church's Fair Share," Copyright 1968 by *Christianity Today*. Reprinted by permission.

4. Fred R. Zepp, *op. cit.*

5. Elwin A. Smith, "Should Church Assets and Income Be Taxed?" Copyright 1968 *The Christian Century Foundation*. Reprinted by permission from the July 17, 1968 issue of *The Christian Century*.

6. "Unbiased Approach" (book review), Copyright 1969 *The Christian Century Foundation*. Reprinted by permission from the April 16, 1969 issue of *The Christian Century*.

Life or Death — 2
Who Decides?

MAN IS FINDING SO MANY WAYS to prolong his days that the mortality rate gets lower every year. It has been the aim of the medical profession to prolong life as long as possible. Artificial respiration has been used for many years to prevent death in cases of drowning or carbon monoxide poisoning. Mouth to mouth resuscitation is possibly referred to in the Old Testament (Gen. 2:7, II Kings 4:34).

Today man has devised methods and machines to save life that by any other century's standards are miraculous. Hospital respirators that give oxygen through the windpipe (trachea) can keep patients breathing and alive for months. Doctors have been using "heart massage" techniques to continue blood circulation for years. Electrical shocks to the heart by a "defibrillator" have saved many patients who suffered from a stoppage of circulation. The electronic "pacemaker," a device implanted beneath the skin of the chest, has saved thousands of lives by providing a regular heart beat. Every year over 10,000 people have these pacemakers implanted in their chests. And, now they are developing pacemakers operated by atomic power that will not need recharging for over ten years.

The means of prolonging life are increasing as

21

medical science advances. Artificial kidney machines and even artificial hearts have been used to keep people alive who otherwise would have died. Organ transplants are fast becoming common operations.

Apart from these rather "conventional" ways of prolonging life, scientists are experimenting and promoting ways of reanimating life. The most publicized approach to date is called "cryogenics" — a process of low temperature storage that can be applied to humans. People who are dying of a presently incurable disease that might become curable in the future, would be frozen to –350°F and preserved until such a time as they might stand a chance of survival.

All these methods, both those now in use and those suggested, have brought man face to face with moral and ethical questions he has not faced before. These advances in modern medical practices have raised such questions as: What is life? When does death occur? Who has the authority to pronounce death?

These questions are of special interest to the Christian because they touch upon basic traditions and doctrines of the church. Many Christians feel that matters of life and death are totally in the hands of God. Men, by interfering with nature's course, are assuming the role of God.

Life, according to Christian teaching, is given by God. God, in the beginning, breathed "life" into man (Gen. 2:7). It is also His prerogative to take life. Job's words sum up this thought. "The *Lord* gave, and the *Lord* hath taken away; blessed be the name of the *Lord*" (Job 1:21b). Solomon also expressed this sentiment when he said that there is a time for every matter under heaven, "A time to be born, and a time to die" (Eccles. 3:1, 2).

If life and death are matters better left to God, who then has the authority to make these decisions forced on us by modern science? When is a person dead? The medical profession had used the criteria of a beating heart as evidence of life. Now, however, evidence of discernible brain waves by an encephalograph is accepted as more accurate. Yet, what about the person who has incurable brain damage, who nevertheless can be kept alive for months or perhaps years? Who decides whether extraordinary measures should be continued to keep alive a person who has no hope of regaining consciousness? Is it immoral to let such a person die? Is it immoral to force a person to live a vegetable existence with no hope for a normal life?

Dr. Alfred W. Price, an Episcopal rector for over 25 years, was asked whether you should "pull out the plug that activates the machine that keeps those people alive and just let them go?" He answered, "In my opinion that plug ought to be pulled, and I rather think that the final word should be the doctor's decision. After all, they are experts in this field. But how does even the wisest doctor know what God's purpose is in these cases?

"Then too, there is the scarcity of beds in nursing homes. Those life-prolonging machines are pretty rare, too. Someone else might need one. I'm sure doctors don't want to be put into a position of making the final decision if they can help it. You may or may not be right — or wrong."[1]

Dr. Price also felt, however, that the family should have a part in such decisions, no matter what their motives. And we ought not to rule out the inexplicable healing that can take place through the power of prayer and faith.

Dr. Willian Erdman, a professor of physical medicine at the University of Pennsylvania feels that *what* we are prolonging should be a major factor in determining whether to continue life. He says, "I believe the difference is in whether you are prolonging the dying process or prolonging life. Unquestionably we should do everything possible to prolong life, but I think when we are only prolonging the dying process and increasing the amount and length of suffering the individual is going through, then we come into the area you have come to talk to me about. I doubt very much if you would have a division of opinion as to whether we should do everything possible to prolong life, assuming that we are continuing a useful and productive life. When it comes to prolonging the dying process, there would be a division of opinion."[2]

Dr. Erdman continues, "We do everything we can which seems reasonable. On the other hand, I think there is a point when it becomes obvious that pumping blood into an individual and keeping a heart contracting, not by its own nerve supply but by electric current, is not really doing anything useful for the patient. The patient's brain may well have died some time ago. But you'll find this debatable and controversial. No man is really in a position to cut off that life-prolonging machine, once it is started."[3]

Another concern for Christians is the question of euthanasia. Many have considered so-called mercy-killing a form of murder. Others deem it as a compassionate act. When the brain function has been permanently destroyed with no hope for recovery, some would consider euthanasia a saner alternative than preserving a person at extreme cost for a hopeless purpose. Many incurably ill people would deliberately choose to die sooner rather than live. A boy in Chicago shot his mother who was dying painfully

24

with cancer, because, as he related, she begged him to put her out of her misery.

Mary McDermott Shideler, writing in *The Christian Century*, advocates mercy-killing on certain grounds. She says that the person enduring prolonged death throes should not have to endure suffering even for the sake of achieving saintliness. She says a person, "should be permitted to lay down his burden before it crushes him completely by producing irreversible degeneration of the mind and person.

"The commandment 'Thou shalt not kill' is ambiguous, if not irrelevant, when the person is already dead or dying in all but the most technically biological sense. The proverb, 'While there's life there's hope,' is inexcusable emotionalism when the only hope left is for death. It may be that in a time to come we can prevent outrages like these."[4]

Perhaps it is a greater desecration of life to preserve a human being in a vegetable state of hopeless torment than to let him die. Society has permitted other forms of death for particular reasons. Killing in self-defense is accepted by most societies. Men are allowed to continue habits such as smoking even though medical research claims it can take as much as eight years off a person's life. Yet we do not permit a person his wish to die a little sooner to avoid his misery.

The goal of medical practice to preserve life is one reason for much resistance to euthanasia. Perhaps doctors have more hope than others. Perhaps the development of possibilities for reviving people who are only clinically dead (clinical death as distinguished from biological or cellular death) in some cases could be an alternative for euthanasia. If brain tissue has not been destroyed, and a person is quick frozen, his body could be stored indefinitely until a time when a cure were found for his illness. Possibly many people with incurable diseases could thus be restored later to useful and productive life.

Robert C. W. Ettinger, who published a book called, *The Prospect of Immortality*, is a principal advocate of the freezing process (freeze-wait-reanimate). He maintains that his "cryogenic interment" proposal is not as radical as it might seem. He points out that it is commonplace to "revive" victims of drowning and heart attacks. The criteria for determining the irreversibility of death are constantly changing. Freezing dying people may be a simple way to preserve for future curability those who are now beyond our help.

Ettinger conceives of his own reanimation into a world waiting for him, which will rehabilitate him and provide re-education. The aging process by then will have been extended so that the life span may reach methuselahistic proportions. Man will finally be given time to reach his own potential — he will be a superman.

So far no one has revived a human being, but protozoa have been stored frozen for years and revived. Hamsters can be subjected to cold of four degrees below zero for about an hour and yet be revived. Other animals have been frozen for short periods and revived. We can't really say it is not possible that a man can be revived. But other questions do come to mind. What are the sociological implications of being revived out of one's context of thought and life? Who decides for a patient unable to make a decision about being frozen? Should Christians seek to extend their lives in this way? How does this process of extending life differ from methods being used today?

Richard Bube of Stanford University believes that

we should view such possibilities as freezing and reviving humans simply as a part of the aims of medical science. We must recognize that God is bringing us to the place where we must make decisions we thought only God could make. The modern physician realizes he isn't expected to leave everything in the hands of God, because he realizes that God works through him.

Dr. Bube says, "The time may well be coming when the basic decisions of life and death are in the hands of men, when man must decide who will be born, who will live, and who will die, and can no longer relax in the faith that God will take care of all things without man's taking up his responsibility and acting. . . . In a real sense man has been brought to the age of responsibility, for he must make those decisions from which his grandparents could safely absolve themselves. One of the most unfortunate attitudes among evangelical Christians today is that which seeks to evade opportunities and responsibilities for action on the grounds that these are areas that men should not tamper with but are in the hands of God alone. It becomes more and more evident that God works out His will in the world through those men who choose to serve Him."[5]

Christians may view man's efforts to prolong and immortalize human existence either as a tampering with God's will or as part of God's plan for man's conquering the earth. Beyond the ethical and moral questions, Christians consider the effects upon Christian doctrine. Even the question, "What is death?" becomes a theological one when related to the resurrection and future judgment. Can resuscitation from clinical death be compared to the raising of Lazarus or of Jairus' daughter? Can man ever really evade that most ultimate of ultimates — the certainty of death?

"To every thing there is a season, and a time to every purpose under the heaven: A time to be born, and a time to die." (Eccles. 3:1, 2a).

"Why shouldest thou die before thy time?" (Eccles. 7:17).

"Why died I not from the womb? why did I not give up the ghost when I came out of the belly?" (Job 3:11).

"Cursed be the day on which I was born; let not the day on wherein my mother bare me be blessed. Cursed be the man who brought tidings to my father, saying, A man child is born unto thee; making him very glad. And let that man be like the cities which the LORD overthrew, and repented not; and let him hear the cry in the morning, and the shouting at noontide, Because he slew me not from the womb; or that my mother might have been my grave, and her womb to be always great with me. Wherefore came I forth out of the womb to see labor and sorrow, that my days should be consumed with shame?" (Jer. 20:14, 18).

Even Old Testament saints had periods of depression when they scorned life and wished death. Perhaps this longing should be considered only as rhetoric, yet they might offer some legitimacy to the cries of those enduring unbearable pain who wish a sooner end.

"For none of us liveth to himself, and no man dieth to himself. For whether we live, we live unto the Lord; and whether we die, we die unto the Lord: whether we live, therefore, or die, we are the Lord's" (Rom. 14:7, 8).

"For me to live is Christ, and to die is gain. But if I live in the flesh, this is the fruit of my labor: yet what I shall choose I wot not. For I am in a strait betwixt two, having a desire to depart, and to be with Christ; which is far better. Nevertheless, to abide in the flesh is more needful for you" (Phil. 1:21-24).

"And as it is appointed unto men once to die, but after this the judgment" (Heb. 9:27).

"And in those days shall men seek death, and shall not find it; and shall desire to die, and death shall flee from them" (Rev. 9:6).

On three occasions in the New Testament Jesus raised individuals from the dead — He extended life. See Luke 7:11-18; Matthew 9:18, 19, 23-26; John 11:43.

WHAT DO YOU SAY?

1. What is the biblical basis for the sanctity of human life? (cf. Gen. 2:7; 3:3, 22). What is the biblical attitude toward physical life? How is it contrasted with spiritual life? (John 10:10; Luke 9:24, 25; Matt. 6:25).

2. In the light of our eternal spiritual hopes, is the prospect of reviving a body that is 70 or 80 years old really desirable? Why or why not?

3. Should Christians be unconcerned about extraordinary measures to prolong life in the light of their heavenly hope?

4. Do Job 1:21 and Ecclesiastes 3:2; 7:17 suggest that only God should determine when a life ends? How do you interpret these in the light of modern scientific discoveries about life and death?

5. Hebrews 9:27 asserts that it is appointed unto man once to die. What implications does this have concerning the idea of reanimation?

6. Are there theological implications of freezing human beings for future reviving? How far should Christians go in accepting the possibility of immortality through efforts to accomplish indefinite extension of life?

7. Do the resurrection miracles of Jesus relate to modern attempts to extend and revive human life?

8. Can Jesus' statement in John 14:17, where He refers to the greater works that those who believed on Him would do, provide justification for modern man's attempts to extend life indefinitely?

9. Should Christians condone euthanasia under some circumstances? If ways to continue life are available to keep a person alive, even though it would be hopeless and extend one's misery, would it be immoral to refrain from using them? Who should decide?

10. Does the fact that inexplicable healings and recoveries do take place give the Christian a basis for rejecting euthanasia?

Notes

1. Pete Martin, "Life or Death — Who Decides?" *Christian Herald,* February 1968. Reprinted by permission.

2. *Ibid.*

3. *Ibid.*

4. Mary McDermott Shideler, "Coup de Grace," Copyright 1966 *The Christian Century Foundation.* Reprinted by permission from the December 7, 1966 issue of *The Christian Century.*

5. Richard Bube, "Frozen for the Future," *Eternity Magazine,* June 1967. Reprinted by permission.

What Should Money Mean to the Christian? **3**

"NEXT TO LIFE ITSELF, money is a family's most important possession." So says Glenn H. Asquith in an article in the *Christian Herald*. He explains, "Money is what is received in exchange for life — money is a form of life. . . . God created all things and gave man freedom to do what he would with the world . . . each one of us barters his life for material possessions and the skills that have come with their use. . . . A man or woman will go to a factory or store or schoolroom and give his life for a certain amount of money. This life-money he stores up to exchange for what he needs — or wants.

"In a family all the income may be the result of the father's going forth day after day to give his life for it. Or the income may be the result of the efforts of several members of the family working. Some of the money may come from gifts, or from bequests from grandparents or others. In any event, not one dollar has come without the loss of life to someone — known or unknown."[1]

One emphatic lesson our entire culture teaches is that money means power. Those with large amounts of money can and often do control industries, educational institutions, local governments or national political figures, and sometimes a local church. Television does a good job teaching that money provides all the enjoyment and happiness one wants. People are portrayed enjoying luxurious automobiles, yachts, fancy restaurants, sporting events, fine clothing — all things which money can buy. Money gives people the power to fulfill their wants as well as their needs.

Paul T. Heyne, a professor of economics at Southern Methodist University, makes these observations: "Everywhere you go today it's a monetary society. Money does not have the power to solve all problems, but in large enough quantities it can make a sizeable dent in most problems. And lots of problems that annoy and disturb people collapse completely when attacked with the power of money.

"That's what we have come to expect in our kind of society. In a highly developed, highly specialized market economy, money is power because it commands resources. By offering money you can induce a man whom you have never met to rise at 4 o'clock each Monday, Wednesday, and Friday and bring 2 half-gallons of milk to your doorstep before you have opened your eyes. Although he hardly knows you, he will be happy to put the milk in your refrigerator if you ask him, and check and replenish your supply of eggs, butter, and ice cream. It's very efficient.

"By offering money you can persuade thousands of people to cooperate in keeping you warm, comfortable, stylish, healthy, and respected. What could be more efficient? By an appropriate disbursement of money you can also please your wife, delight your children, entertain your friends, and even secure the gratitude of the unfortunate.

"Money is power. Every adult knows it — including those who don't have much of it. They know how restricted their power is relative to others who have more money. They know how a lack of money can limit one's freedom: by limiting one's power to live where and how he pleases. We all know this and have taught this diligently to our children.

"Is money bad? Of course not. Money confers the power to be more and to do more. Must we not even admit that, in acquiring money, man is acting out the modern-day counterpart of Adam's calling? He is subduing the earth and enlarging his dominion over it."[2]

Why then did Jesus warn men about the hazards of becoming wealthy? Perhaps there is something inherently evil in money? Why did Jesus say that a rich man (and in comparison to those to whom He had reference many Americans would be classified as rich) would have difficulty entering the kingdom? (Matt. 19:24).

Possibly Martin Luther came up with an enduring answer when he explained the Tenth Commandment in the Large Catechism: "What is it to have a god? What is God? A god is that to which we look for all good and in which we find refuge in every time of need. Many a person thinks he has God and everything he needs when he has money and property; in them he trusts and of them he boasts so stubbornly and securely that he cares for no one."

"The fundamental problem," continues Paul Heyne, "is not as we so easily suppose, something called 'materialism.' Americans are not, in fact, peculiarly obsessed with material goods. . . . This is how we are tempted: personal and family experience, as well as our books, magazines, and television sets, dramatically teach us that money *can* make us free, free to pursue 'the Good Life.'

"We know (at least we Christians know) that money *cannot* in the last analysis set us *free*. But we don't live in 'the last analysis'. . . . we are rather in-doctrinated in the belief that money is god.

"And the problem isn't exactly selfishness, either. Americans are a generous people, by and large. . . . We are touched by suffering, and we do give of our-selves, at least as much as any other people. But be-neath it there often lurks the quiet conviction that money is the touchstone, the balm in Gilead, the ultimate answer to the problems of depressed neigh-borhoods, cancer research, crippled children, and even the proclamation of the Gospel.

"The issue is neither materialism nor selfishness. It is idolatry. . . .

"Jesus said to the rich young man, 'Get rid of all your wealth, and follow Me.' And in that moment the rich young man sorrowfully discovered his god."[3]

In an article, "What Money Meant to Jesus," David L. Luecke points out, "The church has not said much about Jesus' statements on this subject, perhaps because some of the church's supporters are wealthy and likely to be offended. In any case, the gospels, especially St. Matthew, clearly portray Jesus as saying a great deal about money and its power to enslave. Jesus taught that those who ac-cumulate wealth are in constant danger. Possessions tend to possess the possessor. Money can become a major threat to faith, destroying trust in God, love for neighbor, and one's own inner peace and secur-ity. . . .

"Jesus makes clear that the kingdom of God in which the reign of God is established in the lives of people must overcome the other forces and 'lords' which possess and control men. One such 'master' which must be overthrown is the love of money.

" 'No servant can be slave to two masters; for either he will hate the first and love the second, or he will be devoted to the first and think nothing of the second. You cannot serve God and Money' (Matt. 6:24, NEB).[4]

"No piety or morality or scrupulous efforts to keep commandments can overcome the reality of a life wholly committed to money. As long as the man's first love and loyalty belong to his money, he cannot be possessed by God's Spirit. He cannot be happy in the kingdom of God as long as his real king is money. . . .

"In addition, addiction to a 'money standard' of life destroys a relationship of trust toward the heavenly Father and results in anxiety and insecurity. We have already come to understand that in a broad sense whatever one loves, trusts, and fears above all things is really one's 'god.' But money is simply not an adequate god. Men dedicate their lives sacrificially to it, but in rare moments even the money-worshipping man knows that ultimately he cannot 'save' his money and his money cannot 'save' him. . . .

"The money-worshipping man is anxious and insecure; his power and security are no more dependable than wealth. He can lose all at any time. This is why Jesus told His followers: 'Do not store up for yourselves treasure on earth.'

"Furthermore, the money-worshipping person finds it difficult to maintain wholesome relationships with other people, at least where money is concerned. Like other compulsions, money-addiction robs a person of his capacity for love. . . . the love of money gets in the way of love of people, making it impossible for a money-worshiper to maintain wholesome, loving, self-giving relationships with others."[5]

In the light of what money can do and the necessary part it plays in all our lives, how can Christians develop good attitudes toward the meaning and use of money? How can Christians keep from loving money and still provide an adequate living for their families? Establishing Christian attitudes toward money is difficult because of pressures modern life generates to "keep up with the Joneses." (The inflationary economic situation plays no small part in this difficulty). Christians need to follow biblical guidelines in developing their attitude toward money. Being a Christian demands that the use and meaning of money be subject to Christian teaching and not only one's own desires.

What a person thinks about money will affect his life style, his life work, his attitude toward people, his relationship to the church, and even his destiny. Money can be a useful tool to accomplish a worthy goal or it may be an end in itself that consumes a person's very life. Money may be hoarded or given to benevolent causes. It can buy cars or build churches. It can maintain mansions or send missionaries. Christians cannot treat their use of money lightly because all that God gives to them is to be accounted for (Luke 16:2). The Bible stresses that we are to be good stewards of what God gives to us (Luke 16:1-13; Matt. 25:14-30). It is very important to know the meaning and place of money. What does money mean to you?

WHAT DOES THE BIBLE SAY?

"A feast is made for laughter, and wine maketh merry: but money answereth all things" (Eccles. 10:19).

"But Peter said unto him, Thy money perish with thee, because thou hast thought that the gift of God may be purchased with money" (Acts 8:20).

36

"And I will say to my soul, Soul, thou hast much goods laid up for many years; take thine ease, eat, drink, and be merry. But God said unto him, Thou fool, this night thy soul shall be required of thee: then whose shall those things be, which thou hast provided? So is he that layeth up treasure for himself, and is not rich toward God" (Luke 12:19-21).

"Remove far from me vanity and lies: give me neither poverty nor riches; feed me with food convenient for me: Lest I be full, and deny thee, and say, Who is the Lord? or lest I be poor, and steal, and take the name of my God in vain" (Prov. 30:8-9).

"The rich man's wealth is his strong city: the destruction of the poor is their poverty" (Prov. 10:15).

"Then said Jesus unto his disciples, "Verily I say unto you, That a rich man shall hardly enter into the kingdom of heaven. And again I say unto you, It is easier for a camel to go through the eye of a needle, than for a rich man to enter into the kingdom of God" (Matt. 19:23, 24).

"Charge them that are rich in this world, that they be not highminded, nor trust in uncertain riches, but in the living God, who giveth us richly all things to enjoy; That they do good, that they be rich in good works, ready to distribute, willing to communicate; Laying up in store for themselves a good foundation against the time to come, that they may lay hold on eternal life" (I Tim. 6:17-19).

"No servant can serve two masters: for either he will hate the one, and love the other; or else he will hold to the one, and despise the other. Ye cannot serve God and mammon" (Luke 16:13).

"Go to now, ye rich men, weep and howl for your miseries that shall come upon you. Your riches are corrupted, and your garments are motheaten. Your gold and silver is cankered; and the rust of them shall be a witness against you, and shall eat your flesh as it were fire. Ye have heaped treasure together for the last days" (James 5:1-3).

"He that hasteth to be rich hath an evil eye, and considereth not that poverty shall come upon him" (Prov. 28:22).

"Thus saith the Lord, let not the wise man glory in his wisdom, neither let the mighty man glory in his might, let not the rich man glory in his riches: But let him that glorieth glory in this, that he understandeth and knoweth me, that I am the Lord which exercise loving-kindness, judgment, and righteousness, in the earth: for in these things I delight, saith the Lord" (Jer. 9:23, 24).

"Lay not up for yourselves treasures upon the earth, where moth and rust doth corrupt, and where thieves break through and steal: But lay up for yourselves treasures in heaven, where neither moth nor rust doth corrupt, and where thieves do not break through nor steal" (Matt. 6:19, 20).

WHAT DO YOU SAY?

1. In a society where the cost of living keeps going up, how does a Christian guard against becoming a slave to the money-making rat race?

2. What is a Christian standard of living? Should Christians seek to maintain the standards of living non-Christians desire? What are some indicators that a person is living beyond his means?

3. What should the Christian attitude be toward investments? Toward large insurance policies? Toward owning considerable property? Toward retirement plans? Do any of these indicate a lack of trust in God?

4. How much of the money we earn can we rightfully keep for ourselves? Should all Christians tithe? What is a tithe — on our gross income or net income?

5. Is the principle of tithing a valid one in the light of the New Testament? On what basis? In the light of inflation and taxes is tithing feasible for modern day Christians?

6. In what ways can Christians demonstrate to the world that their money can be used to glorify God?

7. Is it right for Christians to spend time investing money wisely in order to be free of future financial worries? When does the pursuit of money become idolatrous? When it is right?

8. Should Christians will some of their money to religious institutions? If so, how should they distribute their estate to their families? Would it ever be right to give all of one's estate to a Christian insituation and none to one's family?

9. Is the pattern established in the Book of Acts where Christians held everything in common a sound economic policy today? What are the dangers of this? What are its advantages?

10. Do the New Testament statements about forsaking all to follow Jesus and counting all things as

loss for Christ imply that Christians should live as poor men? Does the New Testament teach voluntary poverty?

Notes

1. Glen H. Asquith, "Your Money and Your Life," *Christian Herald,* July 1969. Reprinted by permission.

2. Paul T. Heyne, "Is Money Bad?" *Interaction,* May 1967. Reprinted by permission.

3. *Ibid.*

4. From *The New English Bible, New Testament.* © 1961 The Delegates of the Oxford University Press and the Syndics of the Cambridge University Press. Reprinted by permission.

5. David L. Luecke, "What Money Meant to Jesus," *Interaction,* May 1967. Reprinted by permission.

Should We Favor the State of Israel? 4

THE FASCINATING PROGRESS of the State of Israel has captured the imagination of the Western world. Against great odds, it has struggled to become the most advanced nation in the Middle East. It has won three fierce wars to establish itself in hostile territory. Its most recent victory came in the spectacular six-day war of June 1967. But the continual fighting between Israel and her Arab neighbors keeps the Israeli name in the news.

Some Christians have declared the establishment of the State of Israel a direct fulfillment of biblical prophecy. By implication therefore, the State of Israel must receive our favor because it has already received divine favor. What God has established no man dare resist.

But others have been more cautious. They see some fulfillment of biblical prophecy, but believe important prophetic passages have not been fulfilled because Israel has thus far rejected a personal Messiah and has returned to their land in unbelief (cf. Ezek. 36:24-28). Still others see no specific plan for Israel above other nations.

Who is right? What should Christians believe? Should we condone everything that Israel does for fear of divine judgment upon ourselves? Should we take the generally accepted Western position that the

Arabs are all wrong while Israel can do no wrong?

Dr. Newell S. Booth, Jr., associate professor of religion at Miami University, Oxford, Ohio, makes these observations: "The basic question is whether or not Israel should exist as a nation-state. The men of good will accept her existence as right in itself or, while perhaps regarding the original formation of the state as questionable, accept it as an accomplished fact which cannot now be undone. We should not be critical of their taking sides because it is clear that anyone with an opinion on the subject has to take sides: whether Israel should exist or she should not. It would be unreasonable to criticize failure to be neutral in a situation in which neutrality is impossible. What must be criticized is the illusion entertained by the men of good will that they can be and are in fact neutral. . . .

"The Israeli position (which is, of course, the practical expression of Zionism) is based on the affirmation that the Jews are a nation, that Judaism is not simply a religion or a culture but a nationalism which is the inescapable accompaniment of the religion and the culture. Though the Jewish nation was deprived of its independence and then of its national territory a very long time ago, it has not ceased to exist as a nation through all the centuries of dispersions. The ancient injustice of this deprivation must be undone — not simply because it was an injustice but because the very existence of the Jewish people depends on their having a national life, something not possible without independent political existence on a particular piece of land. Jews have as much right to exist as a nation as do Frenchmen or Greeks; if anything, they are more of a nation than almost any other group because of the religious aspects of their nationalism. . . .

"To ask Jews to give up Palestine is to ask them to cease to be a nation, and this is to ask them to cease being Jews. Therefore an independent Jewish nation must exist in Palestine, and no other consideration can be allowed to interfere with this requirement. . . .

"The fact that others live in the area required for the Jewish nation is looked on as unfortunate. The plight of the Arabs who had the misfortune to be in the way has undoubtedly been a source of real agony to sensitive Israelis. Certainly the Arabs must be compensated. However, it is obvious that they cannot be accommodated in any great numbers within the Jewish state. The realistic Israelis, who understand much better than the men of good will the Arab position, know that an Arab population within Israel will always be a potential fifth column."[1]

Dr. G. Douglas Young, director of the American Institute of Holy Land Studies in Jerusalem, says, "The very existence of modern Israel loudly proclaims that Judaism has survived two millennia in diaspora and thus it can neither be decadent nor of no interest to God. The existence of the new State of Israel should force every Christian back to St. Paul's mystery, back behind the sins of the early church so long and so sadly perpetuated, back to the Bible itself where it is clear that God has a continuing interest in Jews. There should come an awakening all over the world, a desire to see the values that God enabled Jews to perpetuate, the values He intends to keep on using."[2]

In the same special issue of *Eternity Magazine* devoted to the problems of the Jews, William LaSor of Fuller Theological Seminary, wrote, "It is probably true that most evangelical Christians are more sympathetic to the Israeli than to the Arabic side of the continuing conflict. If we try to analyze this, there is a biblical promise to Abraham. . . . But we need to think carefully before we decide that the modern Israel and the biblical Israel are identical. A second factor is our common heritage with the Jew. We both derive our faith from the Old Testament, and we both trace our line of faith back to Abraham. A third factor is perhaps the feeling that the Jew has been the underdog, he has been persecuted, he has wandered the face of the earth, now he deserves a place to call his home. . . .

"On May 6, 1967, the 41 members of *Eternity*'s Holy Land Tour gathered in a large room in our hotel in Nazareth, and I tried to answer an important question that had been raised: Is the present State of Israel the fulfillment of prophecy? Little did I think then that one month later Israel's army and air force would be driving back the combined might of the Arab nations, reducing to nothing the boast that the unified Arab states would take back the territory that had been occupied by the Jews, and that I would be faced with a new question: Is this the end of the 'times of the Gentiles.'?

"When we turn to the Bible to study the promises of God, we are amazed by the number of times the land-promise is mentioned, and by the precise detail in which the promise is spelled out. It becomes impossible to dismiss lightly the subject, for it is almost as basic to the Old Testament as is Abraham himself."[3]

But what about the Arab side? Should this not receive a thorough Christian analysis and compassionate understanding? The State of Israel now exists on territory which was owned and occupied by Arabs. Newly conquered Israeli territories have been acquired at the expense of the Arabs. In all fairness, the Arab side of this issue should be considered.

"Apart from the assumption that eventually most Jews will make their homes there, there is no good reason for Israel to exist at all. The real Zionists know this perfectly well. So do the Arabs; they know too that the original Zionist dream forsaw a state that included all the area west of the Jordan and also at least the fertile areas of Transjordan and southern Syria. . . .

"Whether or not Jews constitute a nation is a question that is not in itself of particular concern to the Arabs. But they feel that if the Jews constitute a nation which can exist only by taking land that has been possessed by others for 18 centuries, there is something seriously wrong. They point out that the period from the second through the 19th century A.D., when Palestine was clearly not Jewish territory, is considerably longer than the period from the 13th to the first centuries B.C., when it was Jewish.

"The Arabs ask what kind of chaos would result if every group of people in the world were allowed — even encouraged — to return to the land their ancestors occupied 1,800 or more years ago, displacing those who have lived there in the meantime. They see no reason why the special religious quality of the Jewish attachment to the land gives them the right to push out people who have been its recognized inhabitants for many centuries. They too are attached to the land, and for them, as for Christians, it is also a holy land. They are convinced that if the Jewish religion is such that it requires this kind of injustice, there must be something seriously wrong with that religion. . . .

"The Arabs were not opposed to a certain amount of Jewish settlement in Palestine; in fact, some of them welcomed it until it was clear that the Jewish intention was to take over the country. No group is willing to have its land and its right of self-determination taken from it by foreign colonizers, no matter what religious or historical reasons may be claimed for the action. . . .

"The Jews refuse to accept as a homeland any place except that in which their ancestors lived centuries ago, but the Arabs are expected to accept without complaint something other than the land they themselves lived in a few years ago. Jewish attachment to their ancestral land is widely hailed as a noble thing, while Arab attachment to the land they themselves have lived on is regarded as unreasonable and fanatical."[4]

In the June 5, 1968, issue of *The Christian Century* 62 pastors and missionaries from Middle Eastern countries wrote an open letter titled "Consider Both Sides!" directed to all American Christians. In this letter they stated: "We have an obligation to combat stereotypes about the Middle East. Too many Westerners are surprised to hear of the existence of Arab Christians alongside Arab Moslems in the population of Palestine. Too many Westerners assume that all Arabs are nomadic tribesmen, whereas the great proportion of homeless refugees from Palestine have been farmers, villagers and city-dwellers. . . . One has only to listen in Arab lands to the rumble of tractors and threshing machines (not nearly so romantic as oxen on the threshing floor!) or to the flow of water through irrigation canals and over new dams to realize that the slogan 'But see how the Israelis have made the desert bloom!' is misleading. . . .

"We must try to understand the feelings on both sides. Westerners in general are already aware of what the Israeli feels: pride that he is once more, after so long, master of Palestine, where he no longer need apologize for being Jewish. But Westerners are not so aware of what the Arab feels: resentment at losing his land, humiliation at military losses, frustration at being unable to make his claim understood to the rest of the world. Thus the tendency of the Western press is to call the massive raid by Israel on the Jordanian village of Karameh on March 21, 1968, 'punitive,' while Arab raids into the west bank occupied by Israel are called 'terrorist.'. . . .

"We must challenge the assumption that might makes right. Far from being defenseless, Israel within 20 years has won three wars, has increased her original size fourfold, presently occupies an area encompassing 1.5 million Arabs, has caused the displacement of another 1.5 million Arabs and maintains the most technologically sophisticated military force in the Middle East. . . .

"We must challenge the assumption that Israeli occupation of Jerusalem, and indeed of large portions of Palestine, represents the fulfillment of Old Testament prophecy. . . .

"The State of Israel should be therefore held to the United Nations' resolution of Nov. 22, 1967, calling for a withdrawal of Israeli troops from the areas occupied after June 5, 1967, and for an end of the state of belligerency. . . .

"We urge you to look beyond the one-sided reporting and opinions current in the West, to be sensitive and responsive to the present Middle Eastern tragedy, and to pray and work for a reconciliation which is based on real justice."[5]

William LaSor also points out that "we forgot that the Arab also traces his line of faith to Abraham. We forget that if he is a Moslem he honors Jesus as a prophet. We forget that a large number of Arabs are Christians. And we forget that a vast number of

Arabs are now wanderers on the face of the earth, and they, too, deserve a place to call home.

"Only one who has lived in the Arab world and has talked intimately with Arabs knows how deep are the wounds caused by the formation of the State of Israel. . . . If you ask an Arab Christian what solution he has to offer to the present problem, you will get the same answer you get from a non-Christian Arab: Israel must be effaced, every Jew must be driven into the sea."[6]

Many Christians have rejoiced over the recent successes of Israel over their Arab neighbors. The possibility that biblical prophecy is being fulfilled in our day is an exciting spectacle. For too many, however, their enthusiasm for the fulfillment of prophecy has hindered them from seeing the plight of the Arab people. Those who see only the Jewish side of this question in the light of the biblical promises perhaps would do well to remember that even the Bible doesn't always prophetically paint a rosy picture for Israel (cf. Zech. 14:2, 4, 5, 8, 10, 11).

Some Christians have seemingly forgotten that God loves all men — even Arabs. The difficulty today is: How to reconcile a belief that God has made certain promises to the Jews regarding the possession of their own land (cf. Isa. 11:11, 12; Jer. 16:15; Isa. 60:21; Ezek. 36:24) with the tense political situation in the Middle East — including so many homeless and destitute Arab refugees.

WHAT DOES THE BIBLE SAY?

"For all the land which thou seest, to thee will I give it, and to thy seed forever. And I will make thy seed as the dust of the earth: so that if a man can number the dust of the earth, then shall thy seed also be numbered. Arise, walk through the land in the length of it and in the breadth of it; for I will give it unto thee" (Gen. 13:15-17).

"In the same day the Lord made a covenant with Abram, saying, Unto thy seed have I given this land, from the river of Egypt into the great river, the river Euphrates" (Gen. 15:18).

(See also Num. 34:2-12; Josh. 15:1-12; Ezek. 47:13-20)

"Pray for the peace of Jerusalem: they shall prosper that love thee" (Ps. 122:6).

"I have made a covenant with my chosen, I have sworn unto David my servant, Thy seed will I establish for ever, and build up thy throne to all generations" (Ps. 89:3, 4).

"For I will take you from among the heathen, and gather you out of all countries, and will bring you into your own land" (Ezek. 36:24).

"Therefore say I unto you, The kingdom of God shall be taken from you, and given to a nation bringing forth the fruits thereof" (Matt. 21:43).

"For there is no difference between the Jew and the Greek: for the same Lord over all is rich unto all that call upon him" (Rom. 10:12).

"There is neither Jew nor Greek, there is neither bond nor free, there is neither male nor female: for ye are all one in Christ Jesus. And if ye be Christ's, then are ye Abraham's seed, and heirs according to the promise" (Gal. 3:28, 29).

WHAT DO YOU SAY?

1. What reasons can be given for Christians in the United States giving almost exclusive endorse-

ment to the establishment of the State of Israel? Is this biblical? Is it ethical?

2. Would we condone the taking over of a section of our country by an ethnic (the Indians for instance) group? How can we therefore condone Israel's actions?

3. Is it possible for us to separate our theological ideas about Israel from the political situation in the Middle East? Would we be doing harm to our beliefs in so doing? Why?

4. Is Israel's present return to Palestine a fulfillmen of Scripture? Are any ingredients missing?

5. Should Israel be treated any differently than we treat other nations? Why?

6. What propositions can you suggest to alleviate the tensions in the Middle East? Is war going to be continuous? Why?

7. How can we empathize with Arab Christians in their struggles against Israeli oppression?

8. Why don't we condemn Israel for conquering territories in a similar manner as we condemn other nations that conquer previously unheld territories?

9. If one believes the modern State of Israel is even a partial fulfillment of biblical prophecy, should he be actively engaged in promoting that state's political and economic ambitions? Why?

10. How can the Christian detach himself from emotional involvement in Israel's successes to help present just and ethical answers to the Middle East problems?

11. Will the major powers inevitably be drawn into the Middle East crisis? What support do you give

for your answer? Does the Bible imply this any-where?

12. If you were an Arab Christian, how would you react to Western Christianity's almost universal acceptance of Israel's actions?

Notes

1. Newell S. Booth, Jr., "Middle Ground in the Middle East?" Copyright 1967 *The Christian Century Foundation*. Reprinted by permission from the September 20, 1967 issue of *The Christian Century*.

2. G. Douglas Young, "Lessons We Can Learn From Judaism," *Eternity Magazine*, August 1967. Reprinted by permission.

3. William S. LaSor, "Have the 'Times of the Gentiles' Been Fulfilled?" *Eternity Magazine*, August 1967. Reprinted by permission.

4. Newell S. Booth, Jr., *Ibid*.

5. "Consider Both Sides!" Copyright 1968 *The Christian Century Foundation*. Reprinted by permission from the June 5, 1968 issue of *The Christian Century*.

6. William S. LaSor, *Ibid*.

5 Can Christians Appreciate All Kinds of Art?

MANY CHRISTIANS REGARD ARTISTIC WORKS of the past with considerable reverence. Yet they are highly critical of modern art — even when it expresses the same moral content as older works. In fact, even much of today's religious art has been castigated as being sacrilegious.

One fact often forgotten by critics of modern art is the fact that what are today considered timeless masterpieces were once the contemporary art of another era. Some of them received as great a criticism when they were introduced as present day op and pop art are receiving.

Evangelical Christians have been notoriously uninvolved in the creative arts and the appreciation of their productions. They have seemingly feared artistic expression because it must allow for interpretation beyond the generally accepted literal interpretation of Scripture.

Evangelicals have been accused of being culturally illiterate. They have shown little concern to enter into the world of art and have produced few outstanding men of aesthetic abilities. Some Christians even disdain the use of art forms as a compromising with the world. They feel that God has revealed enough in the Bible for us to waste our time with worldly culture and man-made beauty. Many feel that such thinking has been a hindrance to the advance of the gospel in our "come-of-age" generation. They feel that the disparaging neglect of the arts has built up unnecessary barriers with the world and has robbed many Christians themselves of enjoying the total expression of God's truth.

Frank E. Gaebelein, in a *Christianity Today* article declared, "Some think commitment to the Holy Scriptures as the inspired Word of God and the rule for all of life is a hindrance to aesthetic expression and appreciation. Complete fidelity to Scripture, they say, leaves little place for anything but religious use of art; they consider the arts as generally worldly and thus outside the bounds of biblical truth, mere marginal activities for those determined to be about the Father's business."

Gaebelein observes, "This is wrong in principle, because it assumes a gap between sacred and secular truth and thus violates the unity of truth. Truth, though on its highest level incarnate in Christ and expressed in the Bible, is not confined to religion. All truth is God's."

He continues, "Among the rank and file of evangelical Christians, aesthetic standards are generally low. The evidence is abundant. The pictures on the walls, the books on the shelves, the records played — so many of these things are products of a sentimental, pietistic dilution of the aesthetic integrity that should mark the Christian use of art."[1]

An Anglican thinker, Dorothy Sayers, says in her book *The Mind of the Maker,* "The characteristic common to God and man is apparently (just this): the desire and the ability to make things."

Artistic expression is one of the freest forms of that ability. Often is precedes the creation of more utilitarian objects. In fact, many of the items that we use in our homes were first the artistic thoughts of some designer.

Genesis descries the creative acts of God. Surely He was the Master Artist. The first book of the Bible also sets forth the truth that man was created in the image of God. To say this takes us deep into the nature of human creative ability. In no human activity do we express God's image more broadly than in our artistic presentations.

"Six times the first chapter of Genesis tells us that God looked upon what He had made and "it was good.' Then we read that when creation was finished, 'God saw everything that he had made and it was very good'. . . . There are great spiritual depths in the Hebrew word for 'good' in Genesis 1, and its connotations surely include the concept of beauty. Some contemporary artists and critics today are inclined to downgrade the place of beauty in art. The cult of the ugly has disciples. But Scripture links beauty to God and approves the beautiful. Moreover, by very definition aesthetics is the philosophy of beauty. Art cannot possibly be divorced from beauty. Beauty is inherent in the universe. If the heavens declare the glory of God and the firmament showeth his handiwork, as they so gloriously do, it is with a beauty that transcends in majesty, power, and diversity all the works of men. The problem is that there are many, some Christians among them, whose idea of beauty is not broad enough to include dissonance in music or big enough to go beyond what is merely pretty in painting or blandly nice in poetry and literature. Beauty has various manifestations. It can be strong and astringent; it has disturbing and shocking as well as calm and peaceful moods.

"Man in his making of things follows the pattern

of the mind of the triune Maker of all things. This concept shows us the incarnational aspect of art — its down-to-earth here-and-nowness, in which the idea takes to itself a real body, an actual form, whatever the aesthetic medium might be. In his making of art man does indeed reflect the image of God. To hold this firmly is the best answer to the irresponsibility of those Christians who turn their backs upon the arts as mere luxuries, frivolous side issues that are not to be taken seriously in these urgent days."[2]

"The funny-paper figures of pop art were barely through the rapidly revolving door before they were followed and partially trampled by the images of op art, kinetic assemblages and psychedelic art. This rapid succession of trends shows us that our society is a dynamic one which values the admirable traits of ingenuity and imagination. Many modern artists with fresh, inventive techniques confess, 'I have very little to say. Life is meaningless — at best, a poetic nothingness.' Why should not Christians, who have so much to say, and who acknowledge the Holy Spirit to be the foreman of creation, be the most original, imaginative creators of them all! . . . If our art is not to continue to stagnate, Christians must continually experiment and evaluate styles and techniques. The church must not greet new artistic expressions with mildewed imaginations, but with alert expectancy and willingness to be moved by the unfamiliar. The highest, most noble achievement of art in any of its forms is to inspire worship by compelling compositions to present truth with such intensity that the reader-viewer-hearer will be directed to the transcendent Truth."[3]

Darlene Miller gives an excellent definition of the purpose of art in an article titled, "Art and Our Children":

"The purpose of art is to help us to feel, to see, and to appreciate the world in which we live. It helps us to discover beauty wherever we live. It helps us to discover beauty wherever it may be found.

"Art consists of an artist's statement about his re-actions to some moving experience. This expression is communicated through a design. Reflecting the mind of its creator and the skill he has achieved through a lifelong search for excellence of expression, the work of art is an inspiring record of human achievement. The spiritual values of life can find expression through the artist's creative effort with the world the things of the spirit."[4]

Frank Gaebelein, writing also in *The Church Herald,* had this to add: "Christians today urgently need to rethink their opinions about the arts. They need to do this because the arts relate so directly to the kind of people they are and to the kind of people they want their children to be. No animal really practices art any more than it worships. Sub-human creatures may make beautiful things but only by instinct, and the things they make are not their own conscious creations but expressions of God's thoughts. Only man consciously seeks to express truth through beauty. If life is to be lived in its full-ness to the glory of God, the aesthetic faculty must not be starved. Therefore, the arts are 'a must' for Christians as for all men. . . . The Bible sets forth an exalted standard of worship and gives the arts a real place in that worship. Moreover, when it comes to the common daily use of God's good gifts the Bible is neither repressive, puritanical, nor obscur-antist. It teaches that man and the world about him are God's creation and that all that man has, includ-ing his talents for artistic expression, comes through grace that God exercises according to his sovereign will as he pleases.

"Thus a Christian who looks down upon the artistic faculties or the worthy products of these faculties are merely earthbound and unspiritual does God no honor at all.

"The arts can reflect and deal with the realities of actual human life — man's lostness and sin, the ambiguities and struggles with which he is faced, and also the glorious realities of redemption and of life and wholeness of being in Christ. They can do this not only symbolically but also with a wonderful directness of vision, as in painting or creative writing or in the wordless eloquence of music.

"Nor is it any more becoming for Christians to make a sharp split between the arts and spiritual truth. One of the master-principles of Christian philosophy is this: All truth is of God. There is truth in art, just as there is truth in religion or science, economics, history or mathematics. The Christian who devotes himself to business or science or any other area of life and leaves the arts standing outside 'the house of intellect,' to be invited in only as occasional guests, is slighting an integral part of God's truth. For God is concerned about our use of the aesthetic faculty he has given us."[5]

If Christians are really interested in permeating the world with Christian values, perhaps they should become more involved in cultural and aesthetic pursuits. Christianity so permeated other periods of history that Christian art became the dominant theme of most painting, literature, and music. Can we readily look back upon the great works of art of other days, whether great works of painting such as those of Michelangelo or Raphael, or the music of Bach or Handel, and be satisfied? Ought we not be expressing our faith in Christ in these times through artistic channels that can communicate to our world?

We can't expect to produce meaningful works of art unless we have some understanding of the masters in other ages. And we cannot afford to be cultural obscurantists if we want to influence today's world. There is a wide gap that must be bridged between the great religious emphasis of the past and the secular preoccupation of the present. Christians can help modern man see God's truth as a vital and meaningful element in life by entering into the world of art and infusing it with Christian expressions.

WHAT DOES THE BIBLE SAY?

"He hath made every thing beautiful in his time: also he hath set the world in their heart, so that no man can find out the work that God maketh from the beginning to the end" (Eccles. 3:11).

"Honor and majesty are before him: strength and beauty are in his sanctuary" (Ps. 96:6).

"Blessed be the Lord God of our fathers, which hath put such a thing as this in the king's heart, to beautify the house of the Lord which is at Jerusalem" (Ezra 7:27).

"And Moses said unto the children of Israel, See, the Lord hath called by name Bezaleel the son of Uri, the son of Hur, of the tribe of Judah: and he hath filled him with the spirit of God, in wisdom, in understanding, and in knowledge, and in all manner of workmanship; And to devise curious works, to work in gold, and in silver, and brass, And in the cutting of stones, to set them, and in carving of wood, to make any manner of cunning work. . . . Them hath he filled with wisdom of heart, to work all manner of work, of the engraver . . . and of the weaver, even of them that do any work, and of those that devise cunning work. Then wrought Beza-leel . . . according to all that the Lord had commanded" (Ex. 35:30—36:1).

"And he overlaid the cherubims with gold. And he carved all the walls of the house round about with carved figures of cherubims and palm trees and open flowers, within and without. And the floor of the house he overlaid with gold, within and without. . . . And the two doors were of fir tree . . . and he carved thereon cherubims and palm trees and open flowers: and covered them with gold fitted upon the carved work" (I Kings 6:28-35).

"And God saw every thing that he had made, and, behold it was very good. And the evening and the morning were the sixth day" (Gen. 1:31).

"Forasmuch, then, as we are the offspring of God, we ought not to think that the Godhead is like unto gold, or silver, or stone, graven by art and man's device" (Acts 17:29).

WHAT DO YOU SAY?

1. What is good art? When is a piece of art, whether music or painting, Christian?

2. Can we rightfully produce art for art's sake or for pleasure, or must it always present some moral lesson?

3. In the light of the statement, "all truth is from

God," in what respect can Christians enjoy non-Christian art?

4. If artistic ability is considered to be a gift from God, can non-Christians produce God-glorifying art? How?

5. Is any form or type of art instrinsically evil? Give some examples.

6. Why have some Christians depreciated art? Have they limited the development of competent, creative artists? How can the church develop more creative and aesthetically talented people?

7. Does a painting have to be "religious" in order to communicate the Christian message?

8. How does a lack of appreciation for, and creation of aesthetic material reflect upon one's view of God?

9. Why do some Christians tend to limit creative art? Is it a threat to developed doctrinal systems?

10. Why do some Christians neglect art forms such as drama, ballet, poetry, and abstract art? Are they intrinsically wrong?

11. What can be done to gain a greater understanding of, and use of modern art forms and productions in the church?

12. Are there any limits that a Christian should place upon his selection of art to decorate his home? Should the style of art be a factor or should content be the primary influence?

Notes

1. Frank E. Gaebelein, "Toward a Biblical View of Aesthetics," Copyright 1968 by *Christianity Today*. Reprinted by permission.

2. Frank E. Gaebelein, *op. cit.*

3. Jane E. Lauber, "Is Modern Religious Art Sacrilegious?" *Christian Herald,* April 1968. Reprinted by permission.

4. Darlene Miller, "Art and Our Children," *Christian Leadership,* March 1967. Reprinted by permission.

5. Frank E. Gaebelein, "Christians and the Arts," *The Church Herald,* June 14, 1968. Reprinted by permission.

6 Should We Give Up the Church?

MANY TODAY ARE EITHER PREDICTING or wondering where the church is going. It has become popular for writers, TV commentators and interviewers, and even bishops and clergymen to castigate the church for its irrelevance and lack of social involvement. They invariably predict the church's doom in its present form. Coretta King, the wife of the slain civil rights leader, said that the church was in danger of becoming a "moribund guardian of meaningless ritual as it declines into irrelevance." The demise of religious interest as it appeared in the 1950's has come as a stunning blow to some and a gloomy omen to others.

Recent statistics show church attendance in most major denominations to be down after years of steady progress. Religious attitudes are changing radically. A 1969 Gallup poll reported "one of the most dramatic reverses in opinion in the history of polling." When first asked whether religion was gaining or losing its influence in 1957, only 14 per cent of all persons polled said it was losing. In 1969, 70 per cent of those polled said it was losing ground. This change of opinion is said to parallel the decline of churchgoing in America. In 1968 a poll indicated that only 43 per cent of adults attended church in a typical week. This decline is most dramatic among young people. While national church attendance declined six points since 1958 (the high point), the drop has been 14 per cent among young adults.

Reasons for believing the church was losing ground included such answers as, "the church is outdated;" "it is not relevant in today's world"; "morals are breaking down"; "people are becoming more materialistic." A high school coed gave her reason: "Organized religion has nothing to give me, and I have nothing to give it. The churches today have little to do with people. They don't relate."

Theological seminaries are having a difficult time getting students to enter the parish ministry. Young men in seminary studying for the "ministry" don't think it vital that their calling be identified with a local church situation. Less than 20 per cent in one seminary entered the pastoral ministry in a given year.

People see the church today as an outmoded, disinterested, and decaying institution that has lost its usefulness and meaning in modern society. The church is seen as a self-serving organization that cares more about its own property and status than the critical problems facing the world. It is bent on preserving its own tradition and cultic practices rather than relating itself to the needs of modern man in a changing technological world.

This apparent breach of communications with the world and failure to relate to modern man has led many to the conclusion that the only hope for the church is to radically change its outlook and structure. Church renewal has been a popular word for some time. Many see the task of authentic Christianity as one of removing the obstacles that stagnate the church's true mission. Some would like to abandon the church altogether, do away with all its tradition and begin over.

Well-known religious leaders and theologians have popularized dissent from the established church. The late Episcopal Bishop James Pike early in 1969 announced he was leaving the organized church and joining the ranks of "church alumni." His announced reasons for leaving were that the church no longer related itself to the world at large. Too many "gaps" existed between the church and the world. He viewed his move as the only alternative in view of his own church's stand toward his activities and his theology.

The former bishop of Woolwich, John Robinson of *Honest to God* fame, tells of the possibility of believing in the church being wedded to its institutional organization. He holds that it is an option of Christian ministry to carry on a Christian vocation either inside or outside the church's institutional structures. He describes this position as "creative disaffiliation" as well as "creative affiliation." In a non-religious age such as ours, Bishop Robinson advocates a non-theological ministry. He has suggested that the church advertise to fill the office of bishop to attract "prophetically minded" secular executives.

Many of those who would radically change the church view the task of the church in non-religious terms. They have reacted to the other-worldliness and exclusiveness of the church. They point out that the world no longer listens to the church and then conclude that if the church wants the world to listen to what it has to say, it will have to secularize itself. This generally presupposes ministries that are primarily social in nature. Religious issues give way to racial; social problems overrule soul problems; poverty outbids piety; confrontation outshines conversion. There is an intense impatience with the slow pace of social change. Some ecumenical study groups have even advanced violence as a valid method to initiate social change.

Many affirm that the institutional church only echoes the political establishment and therefore cannot relate to society's real needs. To such thinkers the church is as much a hindrance to progress as the political and business establishments. Therefore, it matters little whether the church exists in its present form or not. To the religious radical the church is useful only if it can help accomplish temporally defined ends. This new ecclesiology resembles the political new left and seems willing to tear down old structures without worrying whether the new approach will adequately answer the problem.

Disenchantment with the established church is not limited to liberal or radical Protestants. Many Roman Catholics are meeting together to have informal masses in homes away from their church buildings and apart from the hierarchy's watchful eyes. These meetings resemble the style of many evangelical churches, with singing, discussion, and informality. This "underground" church is partly a product of Vatican II and partly a quest for reality and meaning in religious experience. There is no solidarity to these groups and no one really knows what direction this "underground" phenomena will take. Whether it will result in a reformation within the Catholic church or work outside of it, no one can be sure. The unrest within the church is real however, and many are willing to make radical breaks with the church in order to remake it.

Rosemary Reuther, a Roman Catholic, writing in *Christian Century*, says, "There is still, I believe, some good news to be proclaimed about God and man. But it cannot be proclaimed for today except through a breaking of Christianity's inherited cultural and institutional framework and through an incarnation in human experience so new, so radically different and so enlarged that perhaps even the word 'Christianity' can no longer serve to define it. It is not a question of liberal gestures by present ecclesiastical systems toward movements beyond themselves; such gestures are basically paternalistic efforts to domesticate those movements on the basis of the old presuppositions. I am talking rather about rebirth of a 'gospel' that can directly and spontaneously mediate new life.

"The pent up creative energy of the Christian communities must be freed to innovate, to discover new forms of life. One avenue for action is the 'seizure' and radical remodeling of an old parish — probably by driving away all the 'church people' and drawing in new kinds of people."[1]

Many evangelicals are greatly disturbed about the problems the churches face. They see the irrelevancy, social unconcern, the suburban syndrome, the culture gaps, the unlistening world and ask themselves what they can do. Some start new churches only to find that people are the same everywhere. Others stay within the context of their local church seeking to renew and revive its mission. Cell groups and neighborhood Bible study groups are developing all over the country. These put new life into churches and challenge the traditional methods of reaching people for Christ.

In 1968, a group of evangelical young men, formerly staff members of Campus Crusade for Christ, drew up plans for establishing "first-century churches." The group called itself "Acts 29" and started churches in homes and colleges, free from expensive buildings, complex programs, full-time pastors and organizational machinery. The group, made up of Christian activists who call for a reformation in the contemporary church, advocate a first-century type church. This movement seeks this either within or without the "organized ecclesiastical establishment."

Most evangelicals do not accept the radical notions that the idea of the church be scrapped and that we do away with church buildings, formal ministries, Sunday schools, and religious services. They recognize that the church has weaknesses, but believe that changes should be made within the context of the present institutional structures. They believe that, "it simply is not true that the church is a decadent, irrelevant institution. The universal church is the custodian of Christianity in our day. And the local church is the focal point of Christian fellowship and the force behind the Church's mission. Much of the criticism now going the rounds is indiscriminate and misleading, grossly unfair to the facts of the Church's history, and dangerous when placed before immature minds."[2]

Rev. Dean R. Kirkwood, writing in *Eternity* Magazine, has a good word to say about the institutional church. His convictions are summarized in these four points:

1. The church as a witnessing, worshiping, serving and learning body of believers is still part of God's redemptive plan.

2. The church needs to know and do God's will contemporaneously without throwing away its heritage for that which today might be considered "modern."

3. The church both locally and globally must provide a broad approach to the life of its people.

4. The church must not canonize theological systems, organizations, ministries or methods, but relate meaningfully the eternal to the temporal.

Rev. Kirkwood further says, "It is in the institutional Church of today that God's Word is still being proclaimed, however inadequately. It is in the institutional Church today that lives are being ministered to in a great variety of ways. It is the institutional Church which still reminds man that there is another dimension to life beyond self, sex, and sin.

"The Church, in my judgment, continues to be extremely relevant for man's spiritual development and his social awareness. Therefore we return to where we began, 'What's wrong with the Church today may be me'."[3]

No matter what one's individual viewpoint, whether liberal, ecumenical, Catholic, or evangelical, modern Christians have to face the hard facts of societal change. It is sheer nonsense for the church to remain stagnant or adamant. Radicals may go too far in condemning the church and calling for a kind of secularized ecclesiology, but evangelicals cannot ignore the rage and clamor for relevancy. We need not change the nature of the evangelical message, but we must constantly re-evaluate our own understanding of the gospel and the manner in which we present it to the world, even if it means questioning the church's organizational structure. It is not enough simply to proclaim the gospel. We must show in practical ways its socially redeeming effects upon individuals and society.

WHAT DOES THE BIBLE SAY?

". . . I will build my church; and the gates of

hell shall not prevail against it" (Matt. 16:18).

"For where two or three are gathered together in my name, there am I in the midst of them" (Matt. 18:20).

"Jesus saith unto her, Woman, believe me, the hour cometh when ye shall neither in this mountain, nor yet at Jerusalem, worship the Father.

. . . But the hour cometh, and now is, when the true worshipers shall worship the Father in spirit and in truth: for the Father seeketh such to worship him" (John 4:21; 23).

"Give none offense, neither to the Jews, nor to the Gentiles, nor to the church of God" (I Cor. 10:32).

"Let all things be done decently and in order" (I Cor. 14:40).

"And hath put all things under his feet, and gave him to be the head over all things, to the church, Which is his body, the fullness of him that filleth all in all" (Eph. 1:22, 23).

"Now, therefore, ye are no more strangers and foreigners, but fellow citizens with the saints, and of the household of God; And are built upon the foundation of the apostles and prophets, Jesus Christ himself being the chief corner stone, In whom all the building fitly framed together groweth unto an holy temple in the Lord; In whom ye also are builded together for an habitation of God through the Spirit" (Eph. 2:19-22; See Eph. 5:23, 25, 27, 29).

"And he is the head of the body, the church; who is the beginning, the first-born from the dead; that in all things he might have the preeminence" (Col. 1:18; see Col. 2:18, 19).

But if I tarry long, that thou mayest know how thou oughtest to behave thyself in the house of God, which is the church of the living God, the pillar and ground of the truth" (I Tim. 3:15).

". . . And the Lord added to the church daily such as should be saved" (Acts 2:47).

"I know thy works, that thou art neither cold nor hot; I would thou wert cold or hot. So then because thou are lukewarm, and neither cold nor hot, I will spue thee out of my mouth. Because thou sayest, I am rich, and increased with goods, and have need of nothing; and knowest not that thou are wretched, and miserable, and poor, and blind, and naked" (Rev. 3:15-17).

(See I Cor. 12:12-31 to determine Paul's attitude toward the unity in diversity of the body — the church).

WHAT DO YOU SAY?

1. Define what is meant by the institutional church? Was the church established in the New Testament an "institutional church"?.

2. What was a first-century type church? Is it an adequate model for us? Were there some elements in New Testament church practices that would not work for twentieth-century Christians?

3. What did Jesus mean when He said, "I will build my church"? Was he speaking of an organization? What is meant when the church is spoken of as an "organism"?

4. What is the biblical basis for the church? Is the organizational structure of the church a matter of

New Testament concern? If not, what implications does this have on the structure of the church today?

5. Can the church exist without some organization? What elements of present day church organization impede the spread of the gospel. How can this be corrected?

6. Paul mentions the following New Testament persons who had churches in their homes: Priscilla and Aquila (Rom. 16:5; I Cor. 16:19), Nymphas (Col. 4:15), and Philemon (Philem. 2). What does this say about early church organization? How does this relate to the present problem of church structure and organization?

7. How does the church viewed as the body of Christ and Christ as Head of the church relate to the concept of the institutional church? Is Christ the Head of the visible organizational church today?

8. Is there an invisible church? If so, how is it to be distinguished from the visible church? What bearing does this concept have upon attacks on the institutional church?

9. Are present day attacks upon the church valid? Are they directed toward any one segment of the church? What should the church do about justified criticism?

10. In what ways does the world view the church as unnecessary and outdated? Is the church really irrelevant or is the world just making excuses for its rejection of the gospel?

11. Do evangelicals share any guilt for the world's criticism of the church? In what way?

12. Have doctrinal deviations in some denominations contributed to the attacks on the church? How?

Does this mean that all do not need to share the guilt for failure of modern Christianity to meet many of man's needs?

13. Has biblical illiteracy within the American Christianity contributed to the world's criticism of the church? Have Bible-believing Christians made their message relevant?

14. How can the church have a missionary or evangelistic outreach without an efficient organizational structure?

Notes

1. Rosemary Reuther, "New Wine, Maybe New Wineskins, for the Church," Copyright 1969 *The Christian Century Foundation.* Reprinted by permission from the April 2, 1969 issue of *The Christian Century.*

2. "Crepe-Hangers in the Church," (editorial), Copyright 1968 by *Christianity Today.* Reprinted by permission.

3. Dean R. Kirkwood, "What's Wrong with the Church?" *Eternity* Magazine, January 1968. Reprinted by permission.

How Should Christians React to Our Sex-Oriented Society? 7

No MATTER WHERE WE TURN we see sex displayed — either as an end in itself or a gimmick for promoting products — be they sexually-oriented or not. "Sex sells" seems to be the theme of Madison Avenue. If you add sex to a promotional stunt, you're sure to sell more of the product.

The present binge on sex has made the facts of life accessible to more of our populous. There is now more openness toward sex and a greater indulgence in sexually-oriented living. This seems to have both its good points as well as its bad ones.

Some sections of the church have been quite reluctant to recognize sex as an important part of life. Many Christians scream "naughty, naughty" every time the word is mentioned. Some still treat sex as evil — as if the sex act were the original sin. They feel that sex should remain in the unmentionable class or in the tightly-locked bedroom. Others believe that the church should either join the enlightened world or do more to enlighten the world. The attitudes Christians have toward sex will definitely tell the world what answer they give to the obsession with sex.

In our sex-dominated culture, Christians must

consider a wide variety of opinions before making their appraisal of what is commonly called the "sexplosion":

". . . we see that God's attitude toward this subject is not one of avoidance, rejection or disapproval, but rather one of acceptance. Why can't the church adopt this attitude too? . . . Let's show a *positive* attitude toward sex because it is not going away, but our young people are — away from the church to find solutions elsewhere. We must face the fact that sex education is taught in the church and the only choice is HOW — with positive or negative attitudes."[1]

"A parish magazine in England recently decorated its front page with a cheesecake photograph of a long-legged glamor girl. 'I think it will help circulation,' the vicar explained. 'The page is meant to be eyecatching. The church cannot stand aloof on the question of glamor. . . .' Actually, the vicar is a latecomer to a game that has been going on for some time. All sorts of enterprising people have been cashing in on sex; indeed, the commercial exploitation of sex through words and pictures has become a pervasive feature of our society. The peddling of eroticism is not a new trade, of course, but its widespread diffusion is new in our day. The massive quantity of sex-exploitative material produced, the unlimited degree of degradation displayed therein, its easy accessibility, the climate of acceptance it has found — these are the distinguishing elements which make today's pornography problem a matter of critical concern. There is meaning far beyond his intent in the vicar's declaration that 'the church cannot stand aloof on the question of glamor.'"[2]

"The United States is suffering from a *sex*plosion

74

— sexploitation being the most popular form of conspicious consumption in the affluent society.

"The sexplosion has two obvious features. One might be labeled simply as sex on the loose. It is characterized by the discarding of many historic moral restraints, earlier marriages, more unwanted babies, more frequent resort to adoption agencies. Among emancipated spirits this complex of activities is generally referred to as the 'new freedom.'

"The other feature of the sexplosion has to do with the official upholders of morality, who stand about either wringing their hands in mild dismay or rubbing their hands in modest satisfaction, and who proclaim sagely that traditional standards for sexual conduct have disintegrated. . . . The only thing new about the situation is the attitude of futility among those who should be the guardians of morality. . . . We have been the victims of the grossest kind of deception. Part of this deception is a fraud perpetrated from without by alleged authorities on sex. Part of it is the folly whereby we have deliberately deceived ourselves with certain rationalist illusions.

"The Big Fraud resides simply in the fact that those who have pretended to be authorities on the matter have been individuals whose personal acquaintance with sex has been slight, nonexistent or perverse, but rarily robust and normal. From authorities of this sort we get one of two emphases: One says that sex is everything. . . the other says that sex is nothing. This is simply a latter-day development of the previous emphasis — a swing of the pendulum from one extreme to the other. As a consequence of this outlook we get all sorts of delightful, carefree literature in which heroes go skipping and heroines go scampering from one couch to another in a sort of 'musical beds' melee; it is always a big joke to discover who is going to end up where, but it really makes no difference — because, as we have learned from *Irma la Douce* and other productions of its kind, harlotry is really just good clean fun."[3]

Amid all the clamor for understanding sex for what it is in our society there are those who warn that there are some precautions to be noted. The sex binge doesn't mean instant enjoyment or that we are on the right road.

The irony of it all is that the kind of sex that has saturated our culture is a caricature of the real thing. The four-letter words which pockmark our literature, movies, conversation and even our thought do not represent sex at all; they are expressions of eroticism which J. B. Priestly says is 'the twanging of a single nerve — to the exclusion of everything else. . . .'

"Sex, in its fulness, is the union of two people, not just two bodies. Almost universally sex is thought of in modern terms as exclusively physical. It is this superficial distorted understanding of sex which has dominated modern thought and which is being 'overemphasized.' Sex, as God intended it, is the interpenetration of two personalities, not just two bodies. Christians know that sex without love is not sex at all. . . .

"Christians, contrary to most contemporary opinion, are the people who know the truth about sex. They have learned this truth because they have faced the prior question of the truth about God, and about themselves. . . . Christians know that sex is good and beautiful, not some mistake of evolution or goof of God. They revel in the knowledge, revealed in the first chapters of Genesis, that God deliberately built sexuality into His creatures."[4]

Dr. Fitch, in his article "The Sexplosion," states, "When we turn away from the frauds and the illusions to the realities of the present scene, one fact stands out: young people today are losing control of their lives. They are having babies when they don't want them. They are getting married before they really want to. They are taking jobs before they are adequately prepared for them. And this is the 'new freedom'! But freedom is precisely what is being lost. There is pathos in the life of anyone who has cheated himself of the freedom really to choose to get married, to choose to have a baby, to choose to take a job."[5]

Rather than continuing the sex binge, Seward Hiltner, professor of theology and personality at Princeton Theological Seminary, suggests that we take what he calls a "bifocal view" of the sex situation.

"Man's sexual nature was not, in the biblical understanding, a 'lower nature.' . . . the Bible sees human sexuality as more than part of man's organic being. As Roland H. Bainton has noted, the Bible sees sex as 'sacramental,' i.e., as helping to perform the purpose of God even if man sometimes does not understand this point of view. 'Sacramental' does not mean that sex or marriage are 'sacraments' in the Protestant sense of acts instituted by our Lord Jesus Christ. It does mean that here, as in some other realms of life, God has a purpose — partly revealed and partly mysterious — that persists despite human ignorance or sin or selfishness. Thus, from this side of the Biblical bifocals, sex is not simply the possession of any human being, or pair of human beings. It too is a kind of stewardship.

"When we look through both lenses of our bifocals, therefore, it becomes equally impossible to regard sex as low or degraded, or to see it as a 'drink of water.' If we regard human sexuality as dirty, or impure, or 'unspiritual' or unfortunate, we miss the biblical position. But at the same time, if we mistakenly believe that we can use sex for any purpose whatever, with no sense of God's purpose in relation to it, and devoid of mystery — then the very human purposes of sex, as God has ordained them, tend to disappear. . . . If God has his own good reasons for creating us male and female, then a part of our grasp of being human is an appropriate identification of ourselves as sexual beings (no matter about sexual activity), i.e., as male and female. . . . A human being is male or female, not simply by biology but more importantly, by association and identification. Part of our humanity is, therefore, this kind of identification, this 'self-location.'

"But human sexuality, because of it is a dual, also teaches about 'otherness.' . . . Rightly exercised and used, human sexuality is a kind of 'progressive school' for learning to get along with other people who are, in this or that respect, quite different from us. At the very least, it is a warning not to try to make all mankind in our own image.

"Aware of the power of sexuality, the Bible was not ignorant of the way in which it could be distorted. It mentions homosexuality and incest and other distortions of human sexuality. It knows that sex can get mixed up with egoistic motives. Paul had to remind the Corinthians that the freedom of the Christian man does not mean license in matters like sex."[6]

What Christians do and think about the sex-explosion might not seem important to the above-35 generation, but it definitely affects the lives of those below that age. The answers Christians give to their own youth in the now generation will have considerable influence upon their development into effective church leaders of tomorrow. With sex being placed far out of proportion and its role being distorted in order to achieve selfish aims, our young people need a wholesome view of sex without becoming prudish. Can Christians take advantage of the present openness toward sex and help offset the bad effects of the modern sex binge? Will Christians respond with firm conviction and constructive thought to meet the needs of Christian young people? What are your fealings about getting off the sex binge?

WHAT DOES THE BIBLE SAY?

"So God created man in his own image, in the image of God created he him; male and female created he them" (Gen. 1:27).

"And Adam said, This is now bone of my bones, and flesh of my flesh: she shall be called Woman because she was taken out of Man. Therefore shall a man leave his father and mother, and shall cleave unto his wife: and they shall be one flesh. And they were both naked, the man and his wife, and were not ashamed" (Gen. 2:23-25).

"How beautiful are thy feet with shoes. O prince's daughter! the joints of thy thighs are like jewels, the work of the hands of a cunning workman. Thy navel is like a round goblet, which wanteth not liquor: thy belly is like a heap of wheat set about with lilies. Thy two breasts are like two young roes that are twins. Thy neck is a tower of ivory; thine eyes like the fishpools in Heshbon. . . . How fair and how pleasant art thou, O love, for delights! This thy stature is like to a palm tree, and thy breasts to clusters of grapes. . . . Come, my beloved, let us go forth into the field; let us lodge in the villages" (Song of Sol. 7:1-11).

"For the commandment is a lamp; and the law a light; and reproofs of instruction are the way of life: To keep thee from the evil woman, from the flattery of the tongue of a strange woman. Lust not after her beauty in thine heart; neither let her take thee with her eyelids" (Prov. 6:23-25).

"But I say unto you, That whosoever looketh on a woman to lust after her hath committed adultery with her already in his heart" (Matt. 5:28).

"But put on the Lord Jesus Christ, and make not provision for the flesh, to fulfil the lusts thereof" (Rom. 13-14).

"Love not the world, neither the things that are in the world. If any man love the world, the love of the Father is not in him. For all that is in the world, the lust of the flesh, and the lust of the eyes, and the pride of life, is not of the Father, but is of the world. And the world passeth away, and the lust thereof: but he that doeth the will of God abideth for ever" (I John 2:15-17).

WHAT DO YOU SAY?

1. Is the present emphasis on sex in our culture something good or bad? Why?

2. In what way does the emphasis on sex as a commodity distort the Christian view of sex? Does the exploitation of sex in the public media take away from its meaning?

3. Since sexuality is one of the basic drives that God gave to man, why do some Christians seem re-

luctant to discuss it freely? Is sex something to be ashamed of, or should we discuss it in much the same manner that we discuss other aspects of life?

4. What attitudes result from viewing sex as "dirty"? Why is this view not a biblical one? What is the biblical perspective?

5. Christians believe that sex is a beautiful and sacred thing. How does this differ from some modern views of sex? How can Christians get wider acceptance of their view?

6. How is the openness and freedom to talk about matters of sex a good thing. How can Christians take advantage of this?

7. What ways are there for Christians to slow down the overemphasis on sex in our society, while still placing proper and necessary emphasis on it? Why is mere condemnation of the world's emphasis dangerous?

8. What alternatives can Christians offer to replace or substitute for the overemphasis on sex in present day advertising? Is there a legitimate use of sex in advertising? Give some examples?

9. What can Christians learn from modern research on human sexual response, such as that of William H. Masters and Virginia E. Johnson in their study on *Human Sexual Response*?

10. What can be done to eliminate some of the perversions of sex that dominate many current plays, novels, and movies? Since the public seems to demand more and more raw presentations of sex, should the church get involved to change this situation? Will obscenity laws help? Should the church advocate and support them?

Notes

1. Virginia Amorde, "The Church Is Teaching Sex," *Christian Herald,* September 1967. Reprinted by permission.

2. Ralph A. Cannon, "Pornography, Sex, and the Church," Copyright 1963 *The Christian Century Foundation.* Reprinted by permission from the May 1, 1963 issue of *The Christian Century.*

3. Robert E. Fitch, "The Sexplosion," Copyright 1964 *The Christian Century Foundation.* Reprinted by permission from the January 29, 1964 issue of *The Christian Century.*

4. Douglas Dickey, "The Truth About Sex," *His Magazine,* June 1966. Reprinted by permission from HIS, student magazine of Inter-Varsity Christian Fellowship.

5. Robert E. Fitch, *op. cit.*

6. Seward Hiltner, "The Biblical Understanding of Sex," *The Church Herald,* May 24, 1968. Used by permission.

Is the Church Widening 8
the Generation Gap?

THE CONFLICT BETWEEN GENERATIONS is a universal phenomenon. Every nation has had to deal with the rebelliousness of youth. The popular phrase "generation gap" does not describe anything new. It simply dramatizes the tension between the young and the old. It speaks of the present estrangement and alienation between the generations that somehow goes deeper than the ordinary rebellion of the young.

A larger portion of the population than ever before falls into the "under—25" category. The sheer number of those who consider themselves the "now generation" is bound to produce conflict. The problem cuts deep into our society, causing considerable conflict and unrest. Today's young people speak louder and make more demands upon society than the youth of previous generations. The "gap" has taken on such proportions that it has become a household word and perhaps has become the scapegoat for many of the world's problems. Yet the gap is a phenomenon that cannot be overlooked or bypassed. Some observers predict that the relations between the generations may become the central issue for the next 50 years, just as the class struggle has been for the last half century.

Perhaps our consciousness of the generation gap

has been heightened by the swift pace of change in our time. Technology and automation have made possible the ability to create a world with fantastic possibilities for good and evil. Instant communication between nations, space feats, news of world events as they happen, horrifying weaponry, the increased standard of living, accelerated transportation — these and countless other facets of society create changes at a pace that doesn't even allow one to keep up with changes within one's own generation.

Today's youth, partly as a result of modern technology, are becoming more intelligent and sophisticated earlier in life. This modern tv-oriented generation is accustomed to the immediate presentation and response to news. It has been deluged with information and is confronted with the cynical truths of life at an early age — perhaps too soon to adequately evaluate such issues without the advantage of mature experience. The "now" people are also impatient with the snail's pace of much of the older generation. It is used to action and immediacy. It rebels when it is told to wait. Youths have received whatever they have desired and cannot suddenly be taught the virtue of patience.

Youth today appear to be more idealistic. They are strong on tolerance, justice, equality, civil rights, freedom and peace. They betray an impatience with the inconsistency and moral hypocrisy of the older generation. They question all tradition and authority and do not accept that which is arbitrarily forced upon them.

The generation gap produces a conflict of authority and values. Youth have acquired a different set of values than their parents. They have been taught to be discerning and have seen that parents and teachers do not practice what they preach. They are quick to detect dishonesty and double standards. They are impatient with hypocrisy and sham. They are less concerned about success and security and more interested in human values.

Their sense of values has made them resent the value system developed by parents under which they are forced to live. They have labeled this burden the "system" or the "establishment." And it is with this "establishment" that they have their greatest authority conflict. Their parents, teachers and political leaders are part of the "system" and therefore are suspect.

No organization or particular part of the system has captured the allegiance of youth. Government, business, education — not even the church — has been able to hold sway over them. In fact, the church comes up for particular criticism because the younger generation knows what the church says in its teaching. Youth fail to see results and action. As the youth see it, religion is practiced by the old as a tedious exercise without much vigor and value. The status quo seems more important than love and justice, and more plans are put into beautifying buildings than helping people. As someone has said, young people are dissatisfied with the church because it insists on having a post-mortem debate about issues that are no longer relevant.

John D. Rockefeller III, said in an article in *Saturday Review*, "Young people today are committed to values of love, human dignity, individual rights, and trust in one's fellowman. These are precisely the values of our Judeo-Christian heritage. The church has been the proponent of these values for centuries. Yet no institution in our society today suffers more from the sheer indifference of the young. By and large, they have dismissed the church as archaic, ineffective, and irrelevant. One young man told me; 'There's a genuine religious revival going on, but the church is missing out on it.' Another said: 'The church could fill a great need in our society, if it would focus less on the divine and more on how to apply Christian teaching to today's world.'"[1]

Young people have dropped out of church in other generations similarly as they are doing now. But it seems that today's youth are more concerned about morals and ethics apart from their religious significance. In many cases it is not what the church is saying, but how it is saying it. Mr. Rockefeller said, "We of the older generation must re-examine our attitudes, our assumptions, and our goals. We must take seriously as do the young the great Judeo-Christian values of our heritage. We must be as dedicated as they in fighting injustices and improving our laws. We must have a sense of responsibility, individually and collectively, for resolving the massive problems of our society. Secondly, we must revitalize our existing institutions whether they be in education, government, religion, business, or politics. They must be made more relevant to today's problems and have a greater sense of mission. At the same time in support of the initiative of the young, new programs and institutions must be developed which can be effective in areas of pressing social need. Fresh approaches to meeting today's problems are essential."[2]

It would be wrong however to put all the blame for the generation gap on the adult world, though adults are the more experienced and responsible. Young people simply cannot blast the older generation and say "you made it this way." They may have to eat such words when they get to be over 25 themselves. Youth should take a good look at themselves and do some evaluating of their own lives. Joseph T. Bayly, writing, "A Word to the Now Generation," admits that his generation has problems but asks the younger set to consider their own predicament.

"We're a mess.

"But what hurts the most is this: So are you. And I suspect that's why you're so bitter about us. You hate to see the mess perpetuated in yourselves. You see your generation going down the same hypocritical path.

"You can reject our hair styles. Our conformity, our ticky-tacky houses, crummy bourgeois tendencies, moral absolutes, music.

"Deep down, don't you wish you could reject the hog as well, that 13 billion-dollar-a-year slice you personally spend? The soft living, plush houses, fast cars you like as much as we do?

"But that would involve sacrifice, poverty, which are things to sing about, not things to do.

"Empty words.

"Do as I sing, not as I do.

"We're fakey, but so are you. You say everything's relative, you want us to look at you in shades of gray — but then you judge us by our own absolute standard of black and white.

"Honesty is your prime virtue, if we hear you right. Then why all the cheating and shoplifting?

"You don't mean honesty like that? You mean frankness, openness about sex and morals, no pretense?

". . . Neither of us is happy, your generation or mine. No hyprocrite ever is. The difference is that we're 20 years closer to the end of the game than you."[3]

Maybe the differences between the generations are

exaggerated. Getting together may not be so much a question of age as honesty with each other. Neither young nor old can claim infallibility; both are subject to the same human limitations.

Oddly enough it is within the church of Jesus Christ where this union between young and old can become a reality. The composition of the church is not made up of just the old or just the young. The church is a group of believers — young and old — who are united in Jesus Christ. They share a common Lord and a common hope.

Of course, being "one in Christ" does not guarantee perfect communion or even perfect communication. The church is composed of humans and a perfect communion does not exist in the church any more than in society itself.

The need within the church is for members one of another to recognize that both belong to the body and are vital to it. Young people are as much a part of the church as older members — they should act as full members and be treated as full members.

Some young people have expressed their concern: "One of the major problems facing church youth of today is that we have no voice of authority in the issues before our local congregation. A solution to this problem would be youth representation at congregational meetings. While we do not expect to vote, we feel that we should have the right to express our feelings on such church matters as the calling of a new minister or the worship service.

"Another problem is that the church does not speak out on many of today's touchy subjects. This is illustrated by the reluctance of the church to give youth any sound guidance in the area of sex. We believe that sex is a matter of great concern to today's youth and that in a Christian community we should be able to get honest, srtaightforward answers to questions.

". . . we feel that far too much emphasis is placed on the idea of a generation gap. It is not a gap. It is merely the normal and natural misunderstanding that comes whenever there is a difference in age, not only in the church, but in the home and the community. Where adults and young people are considerate of each other's opinions and when each looks at the other objectively, the generation gap no longer exists."[4]

When young and old believers get together in spite of their generational apartheid, then the church may be able to help close the generation gap that plagues society. The church must not only take a good look at its attitude toward youth, it must also make a positive attempt to bridge the gap.

"The utmost need of the hour is to confront the protest generation with the person and gospel of Jesus Christ. Only by vital faith in the living Lord of redemption and history can youth find the wholeness, purpose, and power that will enable them to fulfill their possibilities. The Church must spare nothing to enlist its people and pledge its resources in an all-out effort to win the younger generation to Christ. So far its record in this is dismal. Part of the reason for current rebelliousness is that the Church as well as the home has not cared sufficiently for the young. Older Christians must listen and relate to youths in their communities in order to be able to communicate Christ's love and truth to them. And younger Christians must realize that they, more than any others, bear the responsibility of bringing life-giving Christian truth to their non-believing fellows, for young people will most readily listen to their peers. All Christians must help the younger generation to see that only Jesus Christ can deliver the freedom, purpose, joy, and glorious future they are seeking. Believers in him are called to protest rightfully against unrighteousness and to participate creatively in God's concern for needy people and in the building of his kingdom in the hearts of men."[5]

WHAT DOES THE BIBLE SAY?

"One generation passeth away, and another generation cometh: but the earth abideth for ever" (Eccles. 1:4).

"Rejoice, O young man, in thy youth, and let thy heart cheer thee in the days of thy youth, and walk in the ways of thine heart, and in the sight of thine eyes: but know thou, that for all these things God will bring thee into judgment" (Eccles. 11:9).

"Remember now thy Creator in the days of thy youth, while the evil days come not, nor the years draw nigh, when thou shalt say, I have no pleasure in them" (Eccles. 12:1).

"Wherewithal shall a young man cleanse his way? by taking heed thereto according to thy word" (Ps. 119:9).

"Train up a child in the way he should go: and when he is old, he will not depart from it" (Prov. 22:6).

"There is a generation that are pure in their own eyes, and yet are not washed from their filthiness. There is a generation, O how lofty are their eyes! and their eyelids are lifted up" (Prov. 30:11, 12).

"Let no man despise thy youth; but be thou an example of the believers, in conversation, in charity, in spirit, in faith, in purity" (I Tim. 4:12).

"Rebuke not an elder, but intreat him as a father; and the younger men, as brethren; The elder women as mothers; the younger as sisters, with all purity" (I Tim. 5:1, 2).

"Young men likewise exhort to be sober-minded" (Titus 2:6).

"Likewise, ye younger, be subject unto the elder" (I Pet. 5:5, ASV).

"For ye are all the children of God by faith in Christ Jesus. For as many of you as have been baptized into Christ have put on Christ. There is neither Jew nor Greek, there is neither bond nor free, there is neither male nor female: for ye are all one in Christ Jesus" (Gal. 3:26-28).

See also Ephesians 2:13-16 where Paul also speaks of the unity of the body of Christ and our oneness in Christ.

WHAT DO YOU SAY?

1. In what respects has the church contributed to the generation gap?

2. How have the mass media contributed to our present conflict of generations?

3. Was Paul's admonition to Timothy (I Tim. 4:12) about not letting his youth be despised, evidence of a generation gap in the early church? What was Paul's solution?

4. In what way can churches give young people a greater voice in the programs of the local church? How far should this go?

5. How can the church relate to today's generation of young people? How has organized religion made that task difficult?

6. Should the church put more emphasis on its young people? How far should it go in appealing to their life style?

7. How does Paul's teaching concerning the unity of believers (Gal. 3:28; Eph. 2:13-16) speak against the idea of a generation gap in the church? Can churches avoid the alienation between the younger and older generations? In what respects?

8. If "gaps" in life-style and values between the generations are an inevitable element of modern life, what can be done to alleviate the strain and tension?

9. How can the response of adults to the brashness of youth be a bridge toward understanding between the generations?

10. What kind of response of youth toward the ways of the older generations will help relieve the generation conflict?

11. How should the younger generation react to adult apathy and authority? Does respect imply obedience? What is the nature of such obedience? Is it ever right to disobey adult leadership?

Notes

1. John D. Rockefeller III, "In Praise of Young Revolutionaries," *Saturday Review*, December 14, 1968. Copyright 1968 by *Saturday Review, Inc.* Reprinted by permission.

2. *Ibid.*

3. Joseph T. Bayly, "A Word to the Now Generation," *Eternity* Magazine, March 1967. Reprinted by permission.

4. Shelly Davis and Phil Howard, "Youth 'Talk Back'," *The Church Herald*, November 17, 1967. Used by permission.

5. "The Protest Generation," Copyright 1968 by *Christianity Today*. Reprinted by permission.

What about Divorce and Remarriage? 9

CHRISTIANS TODAY ARE SHARPLY DIVIDED on the subject of divorce and remarriage. The differences are between those who hold a strict interpretation of the sayings of Jesus and those who take a broader view of His "exception" clause. A third approach is based not so much upon the interpretations of biblical passages, but upon the practical aspects of how the church should minister to the divorced and remarried people in our society.

With nearly 600,000 divorces taking place annually in the United States, there's a great need for research into and reevaluation of this problem. Many are concerned about what can be done to reverse this trend. They are wondering whether the church has failed to understand the problems and communicate its positions. Has the church failed to translate its teaching into practical terms so that marriage contracts with "until death do us part" clauses have the intended results? How can the church reverse the attitude that even Christian marriage can be a contract with easy escape clauses rather than a commitment without conditions?

In an article, "Death by Divorce," author June Wilson wrote of her personal experience that "divorce is not a happy word, like *marriage*. Marriage is a word like a summer dress — full-skirted, bright, and sunny. Divorce is a strict black coat, high-buttoned against the wind. Yet because marriage happens, divorce also happens. And in the spring morning of life, winter comes in a long, black coat.

"Marriage is no magic crucible which transfigures its partners by some mystic alchemy that they may ever live on a loftier plane. Marriage is an earthy condition between two human beings, not angels. . . .

"Marriage is vulnerable to earthly dangers and maladies. It may happen, as already it has happened to ten million persons in our country, that a marriage can be so stricken it can only die.

"This is the death we label *divorce*. How does the church treat death by divorce? Does it understand, forgive, and comfort? I can better say how the church treats death by dying. . . .

"Today's ministers say divorce is not the answer to anything, but a public admission of private failure. True. But it is sometimes the better alternative to a marriage which should never have been. Then, divorce is the final door out of an intolerable place. It takes courage, hope, and faith to walk through that door."[1]

J. A. Davidson, pastor of Sydenham Street United Church, Kingston, Ontario, declares that "when Jesus said, 'The two shall become one' (Mark 10:8), he was not assuring his hearers that oneness in marriage comes automatically. Rather, he was proclaiming an ideal, setting a standard, and making a demand.

"There is nothing ambiguous about the words 'till death us do part' in the traditional marriage vows. When a man and a woman make that vow together, they are unconditionally committing themselves to a shared life for a lifetime. They are declaring that 'two shall become one' in their marriage and that the two shall continue to be one.

"Some marriages established on Christian commitment do, of course, break down. But this is always a tragic contradiction of the Christian ideal and standard.

"Divorce is sometimes justified between a man and a woman who have entered marriage with a Christian commitment. As the Quaker philosopher, Dr. D. Elton Trueblood, has said, 'There are situations in which it is right to advise divorce, not because divorce is good but because the alternative is so bad.' That is not necessarily a repudiation of the Christian ideal of marriage. It is a realistic recognition that there will be some failures in maintaining that ideal.

"In recent years a dangerous sentiment has become rather widespread in our society. It is the sentiment that rejects the principle of unconditional marriage and which sees marriage failure not as tragic but merely as awkward and inconvenient. It would dismiss the Christian ideal as old fashioned piety, hamstringing bright, modern, emancipated people."[2]

It is also helpful to understand some of the psychological reasons for divorce. These are highly important because many people, even among Christians, give psychological considerations a secondary place when contemplating divorce. Psychologists have found that some people are what could be labeled "divorce prone." They go in and out of marriage after marriage seeking an undefinable satisfaction. Some people, who are really not the "marrying kind," get married. They would have been more satisfied living by themselves — but only discover this after they're married. Some people simply and honestly can't get along with each other — like two south poled magnets, they repel each other. Some lack emotional maturity and find marriage too demanding. Similarly there are those who do not possess the staying power to remain married until that far-off time of "death do us part."

J. C. Wynn, director of studies at Colgate Rochester Divinity School, makes these observations: "The growth of our cities has had a profound effect upon marriage and family living. Divorce, like delinquency, is significantly an urban phenomenon. The impersonal culture of our metropolitan life, the broad pluralism of interests and loyalties, the startling anonymity of relationships which are caused by urbanization — all have a negative bearing on marriage. With the strains of urban living complicated by the affluent sixties, the ways out of marriage actually have increased. People have the city to absorb them and the wherewithal to make the break.

"A related point is the growing economic and social independence of woman. Her ascendency into new careers, better income, the wider opportunities has made her less dependent upon marriage for fulfillment and less entrapped in an unsatisfactory marriage if she contracts one. . . .

"Not all marital failure is weighed in the courts. Millions of marriages in our country remain legally intact while psychologically sundered. Mr. and Mrs. they are in name, but in fact they live in a state of emotional divorce. They are as unhappy as couples who become divorced, yet continue to live under the same roof for a number of reasons — frequently for the sake of the children. They may even realize some perverse psychological reward by staying within a tense and punishing relationship. One partner, perhaps both, may be unwilling to pay the price of actual divorce, a price in readjustment, reputation, and reduced income. Their lives are characterized by separate bedrooms, monosyllabic conversations, and minimal association. . . .

"Marriage counselors and lawyers mutually deplore the courts' unfortunate influence on divorce. In all but a few states, divorce litigation is still founded on the hoary marital-offenses concept of English common law. It requires a bitter contest between husband and wife. One (the plaintiff) sues for a divorce. The other, whether contesting the divorce action or not, is known as the defendant — the same term used for the accused in a criminal case. . . . Out of all the grounds (that is, admissible evidence) for divorce, couples generally tend to agree to cite the least damaging. Three fifths of all divorces in our country are granted on grounds of something vaguely known as *cruelty,* whatever the actual breaking point in the marriage may have been. Approximately a fifth more allege *desertion* as the ground for divorce. . . .

"Altogether, America's states allow for a total of 28 different grounds for divorce. In addition to cruelty and desertion, these include adultery, habitual drunkenness, non-support, and voluntary separation for some specified period of years. . . .

"Marriages can be broken by greater offenses than an act of adultery, we now are realizing. Repeated instances of brutality, immoral acts involving children, and unfaithfulness without sexual infidelity also can destroy a marriage. Thus churches have tended recently to revise their canons and constitutions to take account of the need for forgiveness in both members of a broken marriage."[3]

Divorced people, even though they do find forgiveness through Jesus Christ, seem to find no forgiveness in the church. We forgive criminals, drunkards, dope addicts — but rarely the divorcee. One such person, writing anonymously in *Eternity* Magazine, said, "I have spent much time in talking over my problem with the Lord, and I feel that He has forgiven whatever guilt may be mine in the divorce. But I don't believe the church will ever forgive; I don't believe the Christians with whom I long to fellowship and with whom I wish to serve will ever forgive either.

"I realize that divorce is a scar with which I must live the rest of my life; but must Christians be constantly picking at the scab and making it an open wound?. . . . I suppose some Christians with punitive attitudes toward divorced people are unhappily married themselves, but wouldn't dare admit it. They can't tolerate the thought that they themselves would like to be free of their mates, for that is a sinful thought, so they transfer their 'thought' guilt to one who is actually divorced."[4]

Dr. David Moberg, professor of sociology at Marquette University, says that most Christians treat divorce as an unforgiveable sin — worse than any other sin that people commit. He wonders how many "sinning Christians" are thus lost from churches because of the negative ways in which they are treated.

In a discussion on "What Does the Scripture Say about Marriage after Divorce?" the Rev. Ray Anderson of Covina (Calif.) Evangelical Free Church stated, "In any divorce, it is impossible to say that one is guilty and the other is innocent. It is only a matter of degrees of guilt.

"Therefore, I believe that if remarriage privileges depend on the righteousness of one of the parties, then no remarriage is permissible.

"However, I do not believe that this is the true spirit of Christ.

"Because every broken marriage vow is a sin, I have no right as a minister of Christ to tell anyone — no matter how supposedly innocent they may appear — that they are justified in remarriage. But because Christ said 'Go and sin no more' to a prostitute, I do not believe that I have the right to deny the possibility of remarriage to anyone who truly is repentant and seeking God's mercy and grace."[5]

In the same discussion, Oral Collins of Berkshire Christian College argued that since marriage is a permanent union, the New Testament explicitly prohibits remarriage. "Divorce and remarriage, as well as adultery," he says, "should be seen primarily as sins against the institution of marriage as an intimate and perpetual union, as a corroding away of this moral and spiritual foundation of society."[6]

J. Stafford Wright, principal of Tyndale Hall, Bristol, England, the third member of the discussion group, stated that several New Testament passages justified remarriage after divorce. The innocent party can remarry — attested by the exception clause of Matthew 19:9. If the non-Chrstian separates from a new convert (I Cor. 7:10-16) — the Christian is free to remarry. Finally, Wright emphatically states, "Adultery is not unpardonable."[7]

WHAT DOES THE BIBLE SAY?

"And Adam said, This is now bone of my bones, and flesh of my flesh: she shall be called Woman, because she was taken out of Man. Therefore shall a man leave his father and mother, and shall cleave unto his wife: and they shall be one flesh" (Gen. 2:23, 24).

"Wherefore they are no more twain, but one flesh. What therefore God hath joined together, let not man put asunder. They say unto him, Why did Moses then command to give a writing of divorcement, and to put her away? He saith unto them, Moses because of the hardness of your hearts suffered you to put away your wives; but from the beginning it was not so. And I say unto you, Whosoever shall put away his wife, except it be for fornication, and shall marry another, committeth adultery: and whoso marrieth her which is put away doth commit adultery" (Matt. 19:6-9).

"And he saith unto them, Whosoever shall put away his wife, and marry another, committeth adultery against her. And if a woman shall put away her husband, and be married to another, she committeth adultery" (Mark 10:11, 12; See also Luke 16:18).

"And unto the married I command, yet not I, but the Lord, Let not the wife depart from her husband: But and if she depart, let her remain unmarried, or be reconciled to her husand: and let not the husband put away his wife. But to the rest speak I, not the Lord: If my brother hath a wife that believeth not, and she be pleased to dwell with him, let him not put her away. And the woman which hath an husband that believeth not, and if he be pleased to dwell with her, let her not leave him. For the unbelieving husband is sanctified by the wife, and the unbelieving wife is sanctified by the husband: else were your children unclean; but now are they holy. But if the unbelieving depart, let him depart. A brother or a sister is not under bondage in such cases. . . ." (I Cor. 7:10-15).

WHAT DO YOU SAY?

1. Does the position of your church or denomination allow for the remarriage of either partner of a divorce situation? Upon what Scripture verses is this based?

2. If a person has been divorced and remarried before becoming a Christian, and seeks to hold an office in a church or teach a Sunday school class, should he be allowed to do so?

3. Is it Scriptural to limit the church offices to which a divorcee can be elected?

4. Should a divorced person teach in your church's Sunday Bible school? Why, or why not?

5. Should a pastor ever perform the remarriage of a divorced person? If not, what should the person do? If yes, under what circumstances?

6. Is it possible that some Christian marriage partners are mismatched and psychologically will never be compatible? Should such persons be allowed to divorce? Why, or why not?

7. If a divorcee does not remarry, how should he or she be treated by the church? What about divorcees who remarry? What does the Bible say about this?

8. When Jesus did not condemn the woman caught in adultery (John 8:3-11) was He setting an example of the kind of forgiveness that should be demonstrated by the church? Why does adultery seem to be the unforgivable sin? Does forgiveness of adultery imply any condoning of adultery?

9. If a church maintains a rigid view of divorce and remarriage, how can it minister to divorced and remarried people? Are such people simply to be put

out of the reaches of the church and the gospel?

10. How much of an open-armed attitude should a church have toward divorced and remarried people? Should there be any limitations placed upon the activities of these people within the church?

11. Does the increase in the ratio of divorced persons to first-marrieds indicate that the church is failing to communicate its teachings in the form of practical applicable principles? Can we blame the church for the world's problems?

12. What constructive programs can your local church or denomination establish to help divorced and remarried people? To help the first-marrieds remain happily married? To help all marrieds develop harmonious married life?

ˊNotes

1. June Wilson, "Death by Divorce," *The Covenant Companion,* June 5, 1964. Copyright 1964 by Associated Church Press. Reprinted by permission.

2. Reprinted from the article "The Cost of Christian Marriage" by J. A. Davidson in *Together,* October 1968. Copyright 1968 by The Methodist Publishing House. Used by permission.

3. J. C. Wynn, "Divorce," Copyright 1969 by *Presbyterian Life.* Used by permission of the author.

4. Anonymous, *Eternity Magazine,* May 1966. Reprinted by permission.

5. Ray Anderson, "What Does the Scripture Say about Marriage after Divorce?" *Eternity Magazine,* May 1966. Reprinted by permission.

6. Oral Collins, *Ibid.*

7. J. Stafford Wright, *Ibid.*

Is Total Abstinence Necessary Today? 10

SOME CHRISTIANS SEE NOTHING WRONG with using alcoholic beverages in moderation. Having drunk such beverages without suffering ill-effects, they cannot see why others should make such a fuss about total abstinence. Why should this be an absolute norm for the Christian? There are dangers attached to drinking, but moderates do not agree that these dangers are as severe as teetotalers proclaim.

Thus Christians are divided into two groups: those who feel that it is possible to drink in moderation without damaging a Christian witness, and those who hold that abstinence is the only way to be assured that one keeps himself from the dangers of alcohol and maintains an effective witness.

Those who hold to a view of moderation can find Scripture to back up their point. They show that God has provided good things for man, as stated in Psalm 104:14, 15, "He causeth the grass to grow for cattle, and herb for the service man: that he may bring forth food out of the earth; And wine that maketh glad the heart of man, and oil to make his face to shine, and bread which strengtheneth man's heart."

Paul stated that, "every creature of God is good, and nothing is to be rejected if it be received with thanksgiving" (I Tim. 4:4; ASV).

Those who favor moderation point out that Jesus turned water into real wine at Cana, and drank wine Himself (Luke 7:33-34). He used wine when instituting the Lord's Supper, and the Apostle Paul advocated wine for Timothy's stomach problems (I Tim. 5:23). Some even suggest that Timothy's "total abstinence" from wine was the source of his stomach ailments. Paul told him not to drink only water, but a little wine for his stomach. Perhaps constant drinking of unpurified water, without the alcohol in wine to kill bacteria, was a bad practice. Those who teach moderation point out that while the Bible condemns drunkenness and excessive drinking (Prov. 20:1; 23:29-32; Isa. 28:7; Joel 1:5; Hab. 2:5), it does not demand total abstinence.

Roland H. Bainton, who was himself a total abstainer, points out that, ". . . the use of wine is nowhere subject to prohibition whether in precept or in practice. Jesus was contrasted with John the Baptist who had taken a Nazarite vow: . . . (Luke 7:33-34). Surely this reproach would have been without point if Jesus were consuming only grape juice.

"The temperance interpreters have maintained that the wine into which water was turned at the wedding feast at Cana must have been unintoxicating. But can one suppose that the guests at an oriental wedding, having already freely imbibed, would have considered the last wine to be the best if it were unfermented?

"Finally the wine used at the Lord's Supper must have been fermented unless Jesus was going flatly counter to current Jewish usage. The word *wine*, by the way, is not used in the accounts of the Lord's

Supper. Its presence is inferred from the references to the cup.

"The Apostle Paul recommended to Timothy that he be no longer a drinker of water, but use a little wine for his stomach's sake (I Tim. 5:23).

". . . The only reason I have discussed the matter at such length is that in this country biblical literalists still persist in their efforts to make of the Bible a book enjoining total abstinence. It is argued that since intoxicating wine is a drink of death and Christ is the Lord of life, he simply cannot have turned water into intoxicating wine. There is really no use in discussing the meaning of words in that case. The matter is settled by the presuppositions."[1]

Moderates also point out that the traditional Christian view through the centuries has been moderation. John Calvin, John Knox, and Martin Luther all drank. They were, however, against the excessive use of alcohol. Luther had his "little glass of Wurtemberg beer" while he worked. In Europe drinking patterns are different and moderation still seems to be the pattern among Christians. Abstinence among Christians as a movement began in the United States in the early part of the 19th century when temperance societies began to wage war against the liquor traffic. Their fight culminated in the Prohibition amendment to the Constitution.

An interesting view, which for all practical purposes amounts to moderation, is one called "circumstantial flexibility". Captain William Paterson, an Air Force dentist, advocates this view. He says, ". . . This view states that a Christian is at liberty to eat or drink anything, except under periodic circumstances that would render the use of his liberty unwise, unedifying, or unloving. (See I Cor. 6:12 and 10:23.)

"From a positive standpoint, Christians who hold to this position make much of the 'glorious liberty of the children of God' and rejoice in the goodness of 'the living God who gives us richly all things to enjoy.'

"This quality of liberty demands a wise and responsible stewardship. It depends upon a continual fellowship with the risen Christ, and upon more than a mere proof-text acquaintance with the Word of God for guidance in the ever changing circumstances of life. No mental listing of extra-Biblical 'do's' and 'don'ts' will do for the Christian involved in the dynamics of a thoroughly vital Christianity.

"Hence, beyond God-given personal enjoyment, the Christian seeking to emulate the Apostle's 'all things to all men' is willing to be *flexible* in his performance of custom. On one occasion this may require temporary abstinence; on another he may find that barriers to witnessing-in-depth more easily disappear in the partaking of what is set before him; on still another, he may sense that this may be the time to tenderly enlighten the conscience of a weaker brother, burdened with guilt-producing scruples. And yet upon another occasion decide in exemplary fashion to set aside the moderate use of alcohol before taking to the road. . . .

"It is evident that our Lord did not consider the stumbling of weaker consciences of top priority when He healed and ordered a man to carry his bed on the Jewish sabbath, made wine at a wedding, ate and drank with publicans and sinners, conversed in plain view with an adulterous woman by a well, and publicly criticized the local religious authorities of his day before the multitude. His primary concern was reaching the lost on their level and demonstrating by his conduct that the Kingdom of God was

not a matter of meat and drink, but righteousness
and peace and joy in the Holy Spirit. For it is not
'that which goeth into the mouth that defileth a man,
but that which cometh out,' and in need, therefore,
of the cleansing of the Gospel of Grace."[2]

Total abstainers feel that alcohol is nothing to
fool with. A Christian should be willing to abstain
from all appearances of evil (I Thess. 5:22) and
deny himself even what might be permissible (I
Cor. 6:12). Total abstinence is considered a challenge to a disciplined life in Christ. It is a matter
of conscience and Christian responsibility, based on
love and concern for God and others.

Roland H. Bainton calls for abstinence, not on the
basis of Scriptural practices or precepts, but on
"biblical principles." He says, "The first principle is
this: 'Know ye not that your bodies are members of
Christ? . . . know ye not that your body is a temple of
the Holy Spirit. . . ?' (I Cor. 6:15 and 19). Certainly of themselves these tests do not require total
abstinence. The question is, what does dishonor the
body? Many will hold that a moderate use of alcoholic beverages is no dishonor, but others will reply
that although a moderate use under carefully con-
trolled conditions is no dishonor, nevertheless the
moderate can lead to the immoderate, and the consequences of immoderate use in our highly mech-
anized society are so drastic that one is wise to
preclude the possibility of excess by refraining from
the moderate which may lend to it.

"The second great biblical principle is consideration for the weaker brother. The classic passage is
in Roman 14:

'Let us not therefore judge one another any more.
One man hath faith to eat all things, but he that is
weak eateth herbs. Let not him that eateth set at

naught him that eateth not; and let not him that
eateth not judge him that eateth. . . . Let us not
therefore judge one another any more; but judge ye
this rather, that no man put a stumblingblock in
his brother's way. . . . I know, and am persuaded in
the Lord Jesus that nothing is unclean of itself; save
that to him who accounteth anything to be unclean,
to him it is unclean. For if because of meat thy
brother is grieved, thou walkest no longer in love.
. . . Overthrow not for meat's sake the work of
God. . . . It is good not to eat flesh, *nor to drink wine,*
nor to do anything whereby thy brother stumbleth.' "
Bainton concludes, ". . . For the sake of such people,
those who can drink without excess should abstain
in order to create a social environment in which
abstinence is not an act of courage but accepted
behavior."[3]

There are approximately 7,000,000 alcoholics in
the United States. This figure is increasing at the rate
of 250,000 each year. It is the nation's third most
serious health problem and is costing Americans
billions of dollars. Drinking is the cause of over
25,000 automobile deaths a year — almost half of
the total auto deaths. There is no question that
alcoholism is a moral problem that needs careful
consideration by Christians.

Christianity Today in an editorial entitled "Abstinence Makes Sense" says that the solution to this
problem is found in "voluntary abstinence."

"With all that is being written about alcoholism
and with the sociological, medical, physiological,
and psycological research being devoted to its cause
and cure, there is no secret whatever about a sure
method of preventing it. No one who does not drink
will ever become an alcoholic. Moreover, those who
do not drink, while not exempt from highway acci-

dents, will not be subject to accidents resulting from impairment of their own facilities by even very small amounts of alcohol in the body.

"Surely the time has come for a careful, persistent, and persuasive presentation of the fact that abstinence makes sense. Regardless of differing religious traditions and varying interpretations of what Scripture says about drinking, youth today — and they are the future drinkers of tomorrow — have the right to hear the plain case for abstinence as a valid and socially acceptable answer to the alcohol problem.

"Nothing short of this is fair to youth. Theirs is the hazard, and they must be informed. The reasonableness of abstinence rests on considerations of responsibility, example to others, and the danger of alcohol itself. Many of those who advocate abstinence find their warrant in Paul's words, 'All things are lawful unto me, but all things are not expedient. . . .' (I Cor. 6:12; 10:23), and in his principle of restricting one's liberty in consideration of the weaker brother: 'It is good neither . . . to drink wine, nor anything whereby thy brother stumbleth, or is offended, or is made weak' (Rom. 14:21). Abstinence can only be voluntary. Enforced group abstinence cannot succeed. Nevertheless, to refrain from a practice so fraught with danger and to do so not only for self but also for the sake of others is a true Christian answer to one of the great social problems of our time. Consequently it must be presented unashamedly and unequivocally."[4]

WHAT DOES THE BIBLE SAY?

"He causeth the grass to grow for the cattle, and herb for the service of man, that he may bring forth food out of the earth; and wine that maketh glad the heart of man, and oil to make his face to shine, and bread which strengtheneth man's heart" (Ps. 104:14, 15).

"For John the Baptist came neither eating bread nor drinking wine; and ye say, He hath a devil. The Son of man is come eating and drinking; and ye say, Behold a gluttonous man, and a winebibber, a friend of publicans and sinners!" (Luke 7:33, 34).

"Drink no longer water, but use a little wine for thy stomach's sake and thine often infirmites" (I Tim. 5:23).

"And take heed to yourselves, lest at any time your hearts be overcharged with surfeiting, and drunkenness . . ." (Luke 21:34).

"Let us walk honestly, as in the day; not in rioting and drunkenness . . ." (Rom. 13:13).

"A bishop then must be . . . not given to wine. . ." (I Tim. 3:2, 3).

"Likewise must the deacon be . . . not given to much wine. . . ." (I Tim. 3:8).

"The aged women likewise, that they be . . . not given to much wine. . . ." (Titus 2:3).

"For meat destroy not the work of God. All things indeed are pure; but it is evil for that man who eateth with offence. It is good neither to eat flesh, nor to drink wine, nor any thing whereby thy brother stumbleth, or is offended, or is made weak" (Rom. 14:20, 21).

"All things are lawful unto me, but all things are not expedient; all things are lawful for me, but I will not be brought under the power of any" (I Cor. 6:12; cf. I Cor. 10:23).

"Know ye not that your bodies are the members

of Christ? shall I then take the members of Christ, and make them the members of an harlot? God forbid" (I Cor. 6:15).

"What? know ye not that your body is the temple of the Holy Ghost which is in you, which ye have of God, and ye are not your own? For ye are bought with a price; therefore glorify God in your body, and in your spirit, which are God's" (I Cor. 6:19, 20).

(See also I Cor. 11:21; John 2:1-12.)

WHAT DO YOU SAY?

1. How can Christians today reconcile the biblical practice of moderation with the concept of total abstinence? Do the differences in cultures bear upon this question? How?

2. In the light of practices related in Scripture, is moderation still a valid approach to the consumption of alcoholic beverages today? If so, what particular criteria justify it?

3. What biblical principles support the idea of total abstinence?

4. What is moderate drinking? How much is moderate? What are the weaknesses in this approach?

5. Are the dangers inherent in drinking alcohol adequate reason for avoiding moderation in favor of total abstinence?

6. There are risks in practicing moderate drinking. Are we to avoid the practice simply because of the risks involved?

7. Can a total abstainer be a better witness for Christ than a person who drinks moderately? In

what sense? Are there ways in which a moderate can be a better witness?

8. What should young people be taught about alcoholic beverages? About the merits of moderation or the discipline of abstinence?

9. Is the concept that alcoholism is a disease in harmony with Scripture? Does this concept dilute the idea that excessive drinking is sin?

10. If a recipe calls for the use of wine or some other liquor, should a Christian use such a recipe? Should a total abstainer refuse to eat food that was made with wine?

11. Does the idea of total abstinence deny the biblical affirmation that all God created is good and therefore to be enjoyed in moderation by man? Isn't any excess sin?

12. If moderation is the practice of most Christians in relation to most other things (such as eating, exercise, obtaining material goods), why is alcohol singled out for abstinence?

13. Should Christians support the liquor industry by using alcohol? Should Christians use wine when celebrating the Lord's Supper?

Notes

1. Roland H. Bainton, "Total Abstinence and Biblical Principles," Copyright 1958 by *Christianity Today*. Reprinted by permission.

2. Captain William Paterson, "Christian Attitudes and Alcohol," *Command,* Summer 1963. Reprinted with permission.

3. Roland H. Bainton, *Ibid.*

4. "Abstinence Makes Sense," Copyright 1964 by *Christianity Today*. Reprinted by permission.

Does the Bible Teach the Equality of Races? 11

RACISM IS AN ATTITUDE OF ONE RACE holding itself to be inherently superior to another race. Ideas of racial superiority take hold of a people and become so much a way of life that such people begin to doubt the humanity of those they consider inferior. White racists do not believe black people to be quite human.

This tendency became a mania in Germany during the reign of Adolph Hitler. His national socialism in the 1930's resulted in a mass holocaust of inhumanity. Americans should be particularly sensitive to claims that one race is superior to another. The memories of Auschwitz, Treblinka, Belzec and the Warsaw ghetto are too recent for many to forget how racial pride can beget and justify the most inhuman atrocities.

Perhaps these lessons from recent history can teach us the dangers of holding views that state one man as inferior to another. Whether the reasons be nationalistic, skin color, ancestry, or religion, the seeds of prejudice and hatred begin with a haughty arrogance toward one's own background or characteristic. Whether a person merely knocks a person of another race or simply looks upon himself as somehow superior, he still feeds the flames of bigotry

113

which have separated people from one another through the centuries.

It is a sad commentary on Christianity that a racist temperament has penetrated many Christian groups while they would disclaim racist tendencies such as those evidenced by rabid segregationists in America. Though most Christians often deny outright racist beliefs, they may often subtly reveal attitudes that hint of unconscious racist tendencies. Have we not heard white Christians say of blacks, "They're basically lazy and would rather collect welfare checks," or "Why should we give them welfare so they can have more babies?" or "Would you want one to marry your daughter?" References to "them" and "one" seem to imply that black people are somehow different and not quite equal to whites.

Such attitudes are contrary to the Bible and indefensible. Many Christians justify their attitudes without giving too much thought to the law of love as found in the New Testament.

Jesus exposed the prejudices of those who thought they were better than others. The Pharisees received His scathing rebukes for their exclusivism and lack of compassion (Matt. 23). His story of the Good Samaritan was meant to broaden man's concept of who was his neighbor. He said we were to love our neighbor as ourselves. He commanded His disciples to go to *all* the world — He stipulated that no color or racial line should have exclusive right to the gospel. There is no implication in the New Testament of racism.

Paul said we were not to think of ourselves more highly than we ought (Rom. 12:3) and that God showed no partiality (Gal. 2:6, RSV). He stressed love as a Christian's primary attitude (I Cor. 13; II Cor. 5:14; Rom. 12:9; Gal. 5:22) in relation to

114

men. James warned against prejudice and partiality (James 2:1-7) toward those not as fortunate. John asserted that anyone who hates his brother abides in darkness (I John 2:9-11) and that Christians who ignore good works toward the needy do not possess God's love (I John 3:17). Yet how many times have Christians, because of prejudice, refrained from doing good to those of another race?

The whole tenor of the New Testament puts an end to speculation about God's concern for men regardless of race and the corresponding implication that there are no distinctions of race. Perhaps Paul summed it up best in his statement concerning those in Christ when he said there is neither Jew nor Greek, bond nor free, male nor female, (may we add by implication?) black nor white (Gal. 3:26, 28).

In spite of the New Testament teaching on the subject many professing Christians use the Bible to justify their racial prejudice. Even among more enlightened Christians there are those who entertain just enough "doubt" or "openness on the question" to permit or condone racial aloofness and segregation.

The most common biblical justification used is the so-called "curse on Ham" found in Genesis 9:25-27. This supposedly has something to do with the condition of the Negro people. Religious Southern slave holders used verse 25 to justify Negro slavery, because it said, "Cursed be Canaan; a servant of servants shall he be to his brothers."

Most commentators however reject this view and point out that the passage explains how the Israelites came to a position of dominance over the Canaanites, not the people of Africa. The curse was not on Ham, but on his son Canaan. Furthermore God did not curse anyone — Noah did — and he did so after awakening from a drunken stupor. There is no evidence that God approved Noah's act of cursing Canaan or that he implemented it in any way — and there is no mention of skin color.

According to some, the passage previews some aspects of the Israelites historical development in relation to the Canaanites, the decendants of the Shemites and Japhethites. The descendants of Canaan are mentioned in Genesis 10:15-18. Canaan could hardly be a reference to Ham. Ham's descendants, according to Genesis 10:6, were Cush, Mizraim, Put, and Canaan. Canaan represents only one-fourth of Hamitic stock. The Canaanite races according to Genesis were spread over large stretches of land all throughout the eastern Mediterranean coast. Other Hamitic stock was located in Northern Africa.

The curse itself, whatever its exact significance, more accurately refers to a condition in the Semitic area of Palestine. Herbert C. Leupold in *Eternity* writes: "History explains this clearly. At the time of the occupation of Canaan under Joshua, the Israelites conquered the Canaanites to a large extent. This conquest was completed in the days of Solomon, who subdued the remnants of Canaanites and made them tributary in the construction work of his great temple. So, since a Semitic race conquered the Canaanites, Canaan became a slave of slaves to Shem.

"The other prominent segment of the Canaanites was Tyre-Sidon, or the Phoenicians, from whom sprang the Carthaginians. After a bitter struggle, Rome (A Japhethite race) conquered Carthage (a Canaanite race). That is as far as we are able to trace this historical fulfillment of this word of Noah. . . . Consequently Genesis 9:25 has no application whatever to Hamites other than the Canaanites.

116

To try to make it an explanation or justification of the white man's treatment of the Negro, past or present, is utterly unjustifiable. It has nothing to say about slavery, segregation or racial discrimination."[1]

A more dominant theme found in the Bible is the concept of the unity of the race. Richard H. Bube in the *Journal of the American Scientific Affiliation,* writes, "The first picture that the Bible presents is that the human race as a whole, outside Christ, constitutes a unity. All men have a unity in the fellowship of sin. 'Wherefore, as by one man sin entered into the world, and death by sin; and so death passed upon all men, for that all have sinned.' All men have a unity in the nature of their physical existence. 'And hath made of one blood all nations of men for to dwell on all the face of the earth.' All men have a unity in their spiritual death. 'For the love of Christ constraineth us; because we thus judge, that if one died for all, then were all dead.' All men have a unity in their need for a Savior. 'But the scripture hath concluded all under sin, that the promise by faith of Jesus Christ might be given to them that believe.' Thus we may conclude that the human race shows a unity in that all men are created with the same source of life, of one blood, by the same Creator, in that all men are under the bondage of sin, and in that all men need the same Savior, the Lord Jesus Christ, to deliver them from that bondage. There is certainly no basis in the characteristics of human nature to support principles of segregation."[2]

This emphasis on the unity of the human race in Scripture has strong bearing on the Christian's personal attitude toward people of another color or characteristic. A *Christianity Today* editorial said, ". . . The Church must sound the clear note that

God sees all men as a single race. Racism is wrong precisely because all men must own Adam as their father, even as all believers must recognize that God fashions the new man created in Christ Jesus, the second Adam from above, with utter indifference to race.

"Racism attempts to divide humanity into competing groups on the basis of color. Biblically this is indefensible and absurd. Neither the law of God nor the Gospel of Christ recognizes such a distinction; both are color blind. God himself sees only two classes of persons, the saved and the lost; and the point of division is the condition of the heart, not the color of the skin. Evangelism presupposes the solidarity of the human race, the curse that has come upon every man because of sin, and the universal need or redemption through Jesus Christ. All men love, hate, eat, marry, reproduce, and die. And after that the judgment."[3]

Segregation based on racism cannot be proved on scriptural authority. The exclusivism found in the Old Testament and the call to separation in the New Testament have nothing to do with racial stock or characteristics. It is a religious and moral issue. Israel's conquest of Canaan came about not because the Canaanites were inferior to them, but because they were sinful and outside of God's plan for Israel. God later judged the Jews themselves for their sins against Him. The commands of God not to intermarry with the heathen were never based on an idea of purity of race, but on purity of heart. God wanted Israel to worship Him and not be entangled and polluted by the sinful practices of idolatrous nations. Religion, not race, was the primary factor.

It is, however, in the New Testament where biblical attitudes toward race come to their full significance. Jesus tore down the walls that separated men. His gospel was "for all the world," uniting both Jew and Greek in one body. All men would be equal in Christ as God intended men to be since creation. There are no distinctions in Christ.

The church mirrors the unity of the races by its unity in Christ. What man cannot realize in himself, God realizes in the church. In the church all are one in Christ even as all men in the world are one in Adam. Unity among Christians of all races in Christ should bear a telling testimony to the power of the gospel. "To place separations between Christians is sin; it is sin if the separation comes because of wealth and power; it is no less sin if the separation comes because of the color of the skin pigments.

"In addition to these evidences from the New Testament, we might add one or two more that emphasize beyond all shadow of doubt that saving faith in the Lord supersedes and removes all possible barriers between men. 'For ye are all the children of God by faith in Christ Jesus. For as many of you as have been baptized into Christ have put on Christ. There is neither Jew nor Greek, there is neither bond nor free, there is neither male nor female: for ye are all one in Christ Jesus. And if ye be Christ's, then are ye Abraham's seed, and heirs according to the promise.' 'Where there is neither Greek nor Jew, circumcision nor uncircumcision, Barbarian, Scythian, bond nor free but Christ is all, and in all' Are we not constrained to add, in the present context, 'neither black nor white' to this last verse?"[4]

WHAT DOES THE BIBLE SAY?

"And he said, Cursed be Canaan; a servant of servants shall he be unto his brethren. And he said, Blessed be the LORD God of Shem; and

Canaan shall be his servant. God shall enlarge Japheth, and he shall dwell in the tents of Shem; and Canaan shall be his servant" (Gen. 9:25-27).

"Have we not all one father? hath not one God created us? why do we deal treacherously every man against his brother. . ." (Mal. 2:10).

"And hath made of one blood all nations of men for to dwell on all the face of the earth, and hath determined the times before appointed, and the bounds of their habitation" (Acts 17:26).

"For ye are all the children of God by faith in Christ Jesus. For as many of you as have been baptized into Christ have put on Christ. There is neither Jew nor Greek, there is neither bond nor free, there is neither male nor female; for ye are all one in Christ Jesus" (Gal. 3:26-28).

". . . but God hath showed me that I should not call any man common or unclean" (Acts 10:28).

"Where there is neither Greek nor Jew, circumcision nor uncircumcision, Barbarian, Scythian, bond nor free; but Christ is all, and in all" (Col. 3:11).

"I charge thee before God, and the Lord Jesus Christ, and the elect angels, that thou observe these things without preferring one before another, doing nothing by partiality" (I Tim. 5:21).

"My brethren, have not the faith of our Lord Jesus Christ, the Lord of glory, with respect of persons. But if ye have respect to persons, ye commit sin, and are convinced of the law as transgressors" (James 2:1, 9; See also vss. 2-8).

WHAT DO YOU SAY?

1. How does racism express itself among Christians? Why do some Christians have such attitudes?

2. Does the Bible support racial superiority in any form? What about God's command to the Jews to keep themselves undefiled from heathen nations?

3. Why is racism a sin against God? Why is it wrong for a Christian? What Scripture passages condemn racism?

4. In what way does the biblical concept of the unity of the race argue against racism?

5. Why is the "curse on Ham" an invalid basis for supporting segregation or racial discrimination?

6. In what ways is racial pride condemned in the New Testament? How did Christianity break down the barriers between nations and races?

7. How do political tendencies among Christians (conservative vs. liberal) sometimes influence one's beliefs about race?

8. What are some biblical answers to the racial tensions we are facing today?

9. How can Christians help ease the tensions between races? How important is it that Christians not hold views that perpetrate forms of racism (such as believing that the curse on Ham has some reference to Negro slavery)?

10. Is there a difference between equality of race and the equality of rights? If so, what is it? Is one based on the other?

11. Does the call to preach the gospel to all men imply that all men regardless of race can have equal standing before God?

Notes

1. Herbert C. Leupold, "Is There a Curse on Ham?" *Eternity* Magazine, August 1961. Reprinted by permission.

2. Richard H. Bube, "New Testament Christianity and the Morality of Racial Segregation," *Journal of the American Scientific Affiliation,* December 1960. Reprinted with permission.

3. "One Race, One Gospel, One Task," Copyright 1966 by *Christianity Today*. Reprinted by permission.

4. Richard H. Bube, *op. cit.*

Can We Ever Condone Violence? 12

THE PROBLEM OF VIOLENCE was vividly brought to our attention in 1968 by the shocking assassinations of Martin Luther King, Jr. and Senator Robert F. Kennedy. These brutal deaths have focused our attention on the widespread violence that permeates society. In an era when we talk more about being humanitarians, when theologians have proposed that man will usher in the Kingdom of God, we have witnessed the costliest and bloodiest wars, the most inhumane forms of warfare, the most sadistic murders, and unprecedented methods of tormenting and terrorizing fellow men. We have even rewarded the glamorization of violence in such movies as *Bonnie and Clyde*.

War and the portrayal of violence have tended to harden us to daily suffering and death. Violence has become an acceptable way for society to react to what it disapproves. Some church leaders have even advocated violence as a legitimate means of accomplishing soically-justifiable goals.

The United States Conference on Church and Society, sponsored by the National Council of Churches in Detroit on October 22-26, 1967, met to design a strategy for social action. One suggestion that came out of the conference was the use of open violence as a means by which the church can help to transform society. One work study group released a paper asserting: "One criterion for judging violence is whether or not the violence seeks to preserve privilege based on injustice or to redress wrong. The former is unjustified violence. The latter can be justified."

This espousal of violence first surfaced at the World Council of Churches 1966 meeting in Geneva. There Princeton's Richard Shaull declared that "there may be some situations which only the threat or use of violence can set the process of change in motion."

At the Fourth Assembly of the World Council of Churches at Upsala, Sweden in July 1968, the report on "World Economic and Social Development" stated: "In countries where the ruling groups are oppressive or indifferent to the aspirations of the people. . . the revolutionary change may take a violent form. Such changes are morally ambiguous."

Dr. Robert E. Fitch, well-known professor of Christian ethics at Pacific School of Religion, Berkeley, California, makes these observations:

"One might ask why it is that violence is so widespread in our society today. An initial answer would be that it is an old American custom. It is part of our heritage from the frontier, with its battle against the wilderness and the Indians, and its vigilantes to mete out summary justice. The heritage has come down through the Ku Klux Klan, the I. W. W., the struggle of labor, and the various populist movements. If violence is more culturally pervasive today, we may give thanks to the movies, television, paperbacks, and the legitimate theater — and to all who are the patrons of the excesses there celebrated. Violence flourishes especially under the pampering permissiveness of an affluent society, which understands neither the patience required to work for anything nor the price to be paid for anything, and expects to achieve any end by the device of the timely tantrum. . . .

"Perhaps we must ask again the basic question: What is violence? I find it necessary to have three definitions if we are to cover what goes on today.

"The first and classic definition of violence is that it is injury to persons or to property. In this sense we speak of mob violence and of the violence of war.

"A second definition belongs to a more tough and realistic tradition: violence is the use of force in excess of, or apart from, the end to be achieved. It is assumed that some kind of force is necessary to achieve any end. Violence, then, has to do with the relationship of the means to the end. . . .

"A third meaning of violence — and perhaps the fundamental one — has to do with the nature of the self. . . . Essential violence, then, is anything that obstructs the legitimate functioning of a person: and it can be perpetrated without resort to either the first or the second sort of violence.

"If I am a man who loves his family, and you obstruct my fellowship with my wife and children, you do me a most grievous violence. If I am a teacher or preacher, and you keep me from the use of books and deny me access to a classroom or a congregation, you give me a mortal wound. So also with an institution, whether a university, a draft board, a grocery store, a church, a county court, or an office of the national government: if it is blocked in the activities which constitute its essential functions, than it undergoes an intolerable violence. To submit to such violence is to experience death in life."[1]

Another writer in *The Christian Century*, The

Reverend O. Carroll Arnold, pastor of First Baptist Church, Boulder, Colo., in an article titled, "Fight Fiercely, Christians," pointed out that "violence always claims that it is just. Violence is always, in the eyes of its exponents, defensive. Violence is always rationalized to show that my side is being oppressed, my country is being attacked, my faction is innocent, and mayhem is necessary or disaster will follow. This is the argument of modern exponents of violence, both among those who riot and among the elite guard who shout and applaud and defend violence as the will of God. It is also the argument used by both the United States and Ho Chi Minh in Vietnam. Even Hitler defended his use of unmitigated violence as the last ditch defense of a valiant Third Reich, harassed and persecuted by the European system which would not give it its rightful place in the sun. It is practically the Black Power argument of our day. It is precisely the argument used by every revolutionary force — whether of the left or of the right, whether a peasant's revolt or a military coup — to rationalize its actions. . . .

"The basic validity of these causes is often first-rate, though never and by no means self-evident; but the doctrine of violence which goes along with them can be used by the righteous and the unrighteous, the just and the unjust alike. The Ku Klux Klan, the John Birch Society, The Minutemen, and the German-American Bund rejoice that somebody is developing a doctrine of Christian violence which they can employ to justify their deeds. . . ."

Mr. Arnold previously pointed out in the article that "the back-to-the blood movement is in perfect keeping with our times, and one needn't labor the point that it is popular and well supported by film, by boob tube and by literature from Homer to

Capote. Murder and mayhem have always held a certain attraction, however fatal, but that they should become rubrics of Christian faith is, to say the least, surprising. On what authority does anyone advance this strange new doctrine, 'We must affirm violence'? When that question is asked (which it usually isn't) somebody is sent scurrying for a Bible to dig out that passage about Jesus and the whip and the money-changers."[2]

To understand why we have so much violence, to understand why many churchmen are advocating violence as a legitimate means for gaining socially-beneficial goals, we need to take an honest look at the conditions that breed violence. These include: a war that no one can clearly justify, the inequalities between the rich and the poor, the prejudice against minority groups — especially the Negroes, the impersonality and even utter lack of quality of much of our higher education, the unbalanced sense of priorities by government, the excesses of the arms race.

But these are only outward aspects of the issue. Basically, violence is an inward problem, a problem of the individual's nature. Steven Lemley puts his finger upon this inward aspect in a short article titled "To Do Violence" in the *20th Century Christian* magazine:

"There is more to violence than violence in the street or violence which is a major crime. Violence is not restricted to any race, economic station, or even to an overt act. Striking a man is violence, but hitting out at a man's personality is violence also. When we do and say things which weaken or destroy another's faith in himself or in his God, we have done violence.

"In the home one can do violence to a mate's personality or to a child's personality by bemeaning and belittling words and actions. Personality and character assassination by slander can be violence.

"How do we prevent violence? You may not be able to prevent another from striking out at you with his fist or with his words, but you can turn the other cheek, therey absorbing the violence. About the only thing you can do about violence is to let it end with you. Absorb it and let Christ handle it. 'Vengeance is mine, saith the Lord.' The old saying, 'It takes two to make an argument or a fight' is still true. 'A soft answer turneth away wrath.'

"Look in your own heart for violence in thought or attitude before you become self-righteous about violence in the streets."[3]

The National Observer listed the following causes of violence as stated by noted people throughout the country: "A turning away from religion (Dr. Abraham Heschel, a noted biblical scholar): a glorification of violence in the mass media (psychiatrist Fredric Wertham): an atmosphere of permissiveness (Robert McNamara, a Fordham University sociologist): the growing complexity of life and helplessness of the individual (Avery Dulles of the Jesuits, Woodstock College): the war in Vietnam (Eugene McCarthy): the problems of the poor (Ralph Abernathy): criminal coddling court decisions (Lester Maddox)."[4]

Dr. Frank Pack, chairman of the Religion Department at Pepperdine College, puts this challenge to the evangelical Christian. He firmly believes that the subject of violence in our society should not be left in the hands of liberal politicians or theologians who are simply using it as another tool to accomplish their social salvation. Pack declares that "New Testament Christians must be concerned about violence. By the force of our teaching we must offset this desire for the bloody spectacle among our people. Somehow the emphasis must be changed in our society. We must by action as well as word help men to see the way of Christian love and the futility of hate, war, violence, and man's inhumanity to man."[5]

William S. Banowsky, who has done a considerable amount of research and writing on the subjects of the Christian and the new morality, the Christian and crime, the Christian and the Playboy philosophy, says, "It is self-destructive for one to believe that he has the natural right to do as he pleases under all circumstances. He is soon enslaved with his own appetites. He comes to know that the pathway of apparent freedom leads toward bondage, while the very restraints he has cast aside could have led toward freedom. . . We have clamored for and largely gotten total freedom, but we are now facing a bleak and chilly truth: having flung off one restraint after another, we have not learned how to restrain ourselves. . . . The tragic ordeal through which our generation is now passing was prepared in the long years of easy liberty during which men forget that their rights are founded on their duties. . . . Freedom is not personal; it is social. It is always limited by the fact that we must live together. . . . The time has come to put the defiers of order on the defensive, for the only hope of achieving a better world for all is to work with in the bounds of law."[6]

WHAT DOES THE BIBLE SAY?

"The earth also was corrupt before God, and the earth was filled with violence. And God looked upon the earth, and, behold, it was corrupt; for all flesh had corrupted his way upon the earth" (Gen. 6:11, 12).

"And from the days of John the Baptist until now the kingdom of heaven suffereth violence, and the violent take it by force" (Matt. 11:12).

"Think not that I am come to send peace on earth: I came not to send peace, but a sword" (Matt. 10:34).

"And they smote all the souls that were therein with the edge of the sword, utterly destroying them: there was not any left to breathe: and he burnt Hazor with fire. And all the cities of those kings, and all the kings of them, did Joshua take, and smote them with the edge of the sword, and he utterly destroyed them as Moses the servant of the Lord commanded" (Josh. 11:11-12).

"Thus saith the Lord of hosts. . . Now go and smite Amalek, and utterly destroy all that they have, and spare them not; but slay both man and woman, infant and suckling, ox and sheep, camel and ass" (I Sam. 15:2, 3).

"And the women answered one another as they played, and said, Saul hath slain his thousands, and David his ten thousands" (I Sam. 18:7).

"The Land is full of bloody crimes, and the city is full of violence" (Ezek. 7:23).

"The Lord trieth the righteous: but the wicked and him that loveth violence his soul hateth" (Ps. 11:5).

"O Lord, how long shall I cry, and thou wilt not hear! even cry out unto thee of violence, and thou wilt not save! Why dost thou show me iniquity, and cause me to behold grievance? for spoiling and violence are before me: and there are that raise up strife and contention. Therefore the law is slacked, and judgment doth never go forth: for the wicked both compass about the righteous; therefore wrong judgment proceedeth" (Hab. 1:2-4).

"Ye have heard that it hath been said, Thou shalt love thy neighbor, and hate thine enemy. But I say unto you, Love your enemies, bless them that curse you, do good to them that hate you, and pray for them which despitefully use you, and persecute you; That ye may be the children of your Father which is in heaven: for he maketh his sun to rise on the evil and on the good, and sendeth rain on the just and the unjust. For if ye love them which love you, what reward have ye? do not even the publicans the same?" (Matt. 5:43-46).

"Therefore all things whatsoever ye would that men should do to you, do ye even so to them: for this is the law and the prophets" (Matt. 7:12).

". . . and they shall beat their swords into plowshares, and their spears into pruninghooks: nation shall not lift up a sword against nation, neither shall they learn war anymore" (Micah 4:3).

"Then said Jesus unto him, Put up again thy sword into his place: for all they that take the sword shall perish with the sword" (Matt. 26:52).

WHAT DO YOU SAY?

1. In the Old Testament violence (war) was a way for Israel to gain its ends and to maintain its status in the world. How do you answer critics who conclude that the Bible condones violence?

2. How do you answer the person who honestly questions why God couldn't have led the people of Israel by some other means than violence in solving their problems with enemies and neighbors? How can we explain the commands in the Old Testament to use violence to destroy enemies?

3. Paul said, "Let us therefore follow after the things which make for peace" (Rom. 14:19). Why do many conservative Christians almost unquestioningly support our country's war efforts?

4. How can we justify support of violence in a war in a far-off country, but not the right to resort to violence to gain domestic social goals?

5. What workable alternatives can be offered to those in city ghettos who do not have the political or financial power to overcome poverty and injustice?

6. Is it as much an act of violence for someone to take advantage of those in the ghetto as it is for those in the ghetto to lash back?

7. Since the majority of Americans reject violence as a legitimate method of social action, what methods can Christians use that will help bring about necessary social reforms?

8. If violence is to be opposed, why do some Christians avoid and even oppose non-violent movements that operate in our country? If we believe in non-violent means to gain desired ends, why aren't evangelical Christians more active in such movements?

9. How can the Christian actively demonstrate that the way of love is superior to the way of violence in the areas of social reform that are needed in our country?

10. Should a Christian be a conscientious objector and a pacifist? Should a Christian ever support war?

11. Can a Christian condone violence in self defense, or in defense of a loved one? If so, why not also in defense of justice? of your country?

Notes

1. Robert E. Fitch, "The Uses of Violence," Copyright 1968 *The Christian Century Foundation*. Reprinted by permission from the April 17, 1968 issue of *The Christian Century*.

2. O. Carroll Arnold, "Fight Fiercely, Christian," Copyright 1968 *The Christian Century Foundation*. Reprinted by permission from the June 19, 1968 issue of *The Christian Century*.

3. Steven Lemley, "To Do Violence," *20th Century Christian*, September 1968. Reprinted with permission.

4. "Violence Rooted Deep in the U.S., But So Is Reverence for the Law," *The National Observer*, June 10, 1968. Reprinted with permission.

5. Frank Pack, "Shall We Glorify Violence?" *20th Century Christian*, September 1968. Reprinted with permission.

6. William S. Banowsky, "Freedom Is Never Free," a pamphlet published by the author, 1121 West 79th St., Los Angeles, California 90044. Reprinted with permission.

13 Why Be Physically Fit?

SELDOM IN THE HISTORY of the world have so many people been encouraged to be physically fit. Americans probably receive more advice and admonition to keep physically fit than most people in the world. Television, radio, books, magazines and other mass media encourage Americans to jog, stop smoking, stay thin, and lose excess weight. A new diet scheme appears in print almost daily. Home reducing machines, exercise kits, and ten-day wonder diets abound. Exercise is held out to be the cure-all for many of man's physical and mental problems.

Physical fitness has become a national mania. You see joggers in parks and along streets; gymnasiums and health clubs are overcrowded; people are dancing, hopping, kicking — all for the sake of fitness. Sales of bicycles, slant boards, bar bells, and other muscle builders and toners come close to $40 million yearly. Exercise books have become overnight bestsellers. Since 1963, the United States government pamphlet on *Adult Physical Fitness* has sold over 750,000 copies without advertising. Television, with it's daily calisthenics programs, has made its contribution to the physical fitness fad.

In spite of all the bombardment from the nation's advertisers and health advocates, millions of Americans are overweight, physically weak, and generally out of shape. In spite of diet food and drink commercials on TV, Americans still eat too much, sit too much, and weigh too much. Automobiles, elevators, drive-in restaurants, banks, laundromats, and other labor saving factors may have given people more time, but they also contribute to our increased numbers of heart attacks, increased tension and nervous problems.

Recent studies have shown the relationship between inactivity and certain physical diseases and ailments. They have proven the relationship of smoking to lung cancer, emphysema, and other respiratory problems. High blood pressure and high cholesterol counts, both detrimental to health, have been connected with inactivity and lack of exercise. The importance of maintaining physical exercise and proper diet have been shown to have a significant affect on mental and emotional health.

Americans are great lovers of substitutes. They like to enjoy the pleasures of life without having to pay the consequences. So they consume more and more synthetic foods and sugarless soda to satisfy their passion to eat and drink. Then they take diet pills to curtail appetite. This makes them tense so they eat more, smoke more and relax less. The endless fight goes on and on.

Good health requires discipline, good sense, and moderation. Very few argue against the benefits of exercise and a physical fitness program for maintaining good health. Yet very few really take the time to become physically fit. In fact, many are confused about what being physically fit really means. Some consider "feeling good" as physical fitness. Others guage their fitness by their ability to participate in active sports. Obviously physical fitness doesn't mean the same thing to everyone. The American Medical Association defines it as the "general capacity to respond favorably to physical effort."

Whatever one's individual approach to keeping physically fit, the end result remains the important fact. Physical fitness is desirable not as an end in itself, but for its total effect upon a person's physical, mental, and spiritual well-being.

Former President John F. Kennedy said, "Physical fitness is not only one of the most important keys to a healthy body, it is the basis of dynamic and creative intellectual activity. The relationship between the soundness of the body and the activities of mind is subtle and complex. Much is not yet understood. But we do know that the Greeks knew: That intelligence and skill can only function at the peak of their capacity when the body is healthy and strong; that hardy spirits and tough minds usually inhabit sound bodies."[1]

Christians who are generally concerned with the state of their spiritual condition might ask what all this means for them? Does God expect us to spend time nurturing and developing our physical bodies? Is not all this fuss about fitness really an unnecessary and time-consuming activity that can better be spent in spiritual exercises? After all, the Bible says, "Bodily exercise profiteth little: but godliness is profitable unto all things" (I Tim. 4:8).

The evidence modern research has produced, however, brings into focus an important consideration. Physical fitness seems to have a definite relationship to a person's psychological make up — a vital element in a Christian's overall spiritual dynamic. The Bible stresses the importance of the body as it relates to the spiritual life. Jesus warned against letting any part of the body offend or interfere in a person's obedience to God (Matt. 5:29, 30). The Apostle Paul said that he disciplined his body to avoid disqualification in his ministry (I Cor. 9:26, 27). He taught that the Christian's body was God's sanctuary and that He would punish those who defiled His temple (I Cor. 3:16, 17). He taught that Christians should glorify God in their bodies and spirits (I Cor. 6:19, 20), and intimated that while spiritual growth was a primary consideration for the Christian, bodily fitness was of some value (cf. I Tim. 4:8, Phillips). The implications of these references point to an interaction between body and spirit, a relationship that cannot be ignored when one considers his total commitment to God.

While Scripture recognizes the limitations of the body and its propensity to seek satisfaction in carnal desires, it does not regard the body as the sole cause of sin. The Bible attributes sin to the mind of man (Rom. 1:28; Eph. 4:17; Titus 1:15; II Cor. 3:14; II Cor. 4:4) not only to the fleshly desires of the body. Sin corrupts the total personality.

The Greek philosophers attributed all evil to matter. They considered the body innately evil while the mind was essentially free of sin. As long as the mind was encased in the body it too was under the sway of evil. Only when the mind was free of the body would it be free of evil. Those in the early church who adopted Greek ideas about matter were partly responsible for the erroneous views that generated ascetic, monastic, and celibate practices among Christians. These attitudes still crop up among some Christian people who hesitate to enjoy healthful and legitimate bodily pleasures. The frequent attitude that "if it feels good it must be wrong" may possibly stem from such ancient Greek ideas. The Bible never justifies overindulgence or bodily satisfaction that hinders godliness and holy living. The Bible condemns using the body only for self gratification. It not only condemns such things as excessive appetite for sex and alcohol, but also excessive appetite for food, a vice called gluttony (Prov. 23:21, Phil. 3:19).

The Bible condemns abuses to the body, not healthful and legitimate use of the body. Paul's allusions to the Greek races and his comparison of these events to the Christian life show his acquaintance with, and perhaps even his enjoyment of, various competitive games. To be sure there is no direct command in Scripture to exercise or jog, but we should bear in mind that the physical demands on the lives of biblical people afforded natural exercise that we moderns do not enjoy. While they walked everywhere, we drive or ride. While they expended physical effort in their daily tasks, we press buttons and pull levers. They were peripatetic — we are sedentary. Nor did they have all the advantages of modern science and medicine to keep their bodies healthy. Sickness and disease took their lives not because they abused their bodies so much as the conditions of their times made them vulnerable. With modern medical advantages we do not die from the same diseases, yet deaths and disabilities related to lack of exercise and general bodily fitness reach epidemic proportions. Diseases of the heart are the leading cause of death in the United States. They account for 39% of all deaths. Cardiovascular diseases altogether account for about 55% of all deaths. Almost one million deaths a year stem from heart and respiratory problems.

Statistics do not tell the whole story, but these figures coupled with medical research on the causes of heart and respiratory diseases give enough weight to the conclusion that good health, sensible exercise, and proper eating habits go a long way toward a long and happy life. There is no reason in the world that Christians shouldn't make the most of it (cf. John 10:10).

WHAT DOES THE BIBLE SAY?

"For bodily exercise profiteth little: but godliness is profitable unto all things. . ." (I Tim. 4:8).

"But I keep under my body, and bring it unto subjection: lest that by any means, when I have preached to others, I myself should be a castaway" (I Cor. 9:27).

"Know ye not that ye are the temple of God, and that the Spirit of God dwelleth in you? If any man defile the temple of God, him shall God destroy; for the temple of God is holy, which temple ye are" (I Cor. 3:16, 17).

"What? know ye not that your body is the temple of the Holy Ghost which is in you, which ye have of God, and ye are not your own? For ye are bought with a price: therefore glorify God in your body, and in your spirit, which are God's (I Cor. 6:19, 20).

"For our conversation is in heaven; from whence also we look for the Saviour, the Lord Jesus Christ: Who shall change our vile body, that it may be fashioned like unto his glorious body, according to the working whereby he is able even to subdue all things unto himself" (Phil. 3:20, 21).

WHAT DO YOU SAY?

1. How would you define physical fitness?

2. What is the Christian view of the body? Is the body to be considered sinful?

3. What are the implications of the Apostle Paul's attitude concerning sports and bodily fitness? How does Paul's concept of the body as the temple of God relate to physical fitness?

4. Why can indifference toward physical fitness and bodily exercise be considered sinful?

5. Compare the physical activities of Jesus and His disciples. How did their normal physical activity differ from ours? Why do we need to supplement our physical activity?

6. Can a person be a better Christian if he exercises and is physically fit? In what respect? Can passion for fitness be a hindrance to the Christian? In what respect?

7. Would some Christians have better attitude toward life if they followed some form of exercise? Why?

8. Are any forms of exercise — such as yoga, karate or judo — questionable practices for the Christian? What guidelines should Christians follow in choosing various forms of exercise?

9. Does the well-being of the body have any affect on the well-being of the soul? Does the well-being of the soul have any affect on the condition of the body?

Notes

1. J. F. Kennedy, "The Soft American," *Sports Illustrated*, December 26, 1960. Reprinted with permission.